GRILL IT IN!

RECIPES
FOR THE
STOVETOP GRILL

Barbara Grunes

101 Productions/The Cole Group
Santa Rosa, California

Publisher	Brete C. Harrison
Associate Publisher	James Connolly
Editors	Annette Gooch, Susanne Fitzpatrick, and Anna Morgan
Proofreader	Carolyn Chandler
Cover Design	Glenn Martinez and Associates
Interior Designers	Linda Hauck and Charlene Johnson
Illustrator	John Boskovich

Although developed using the Burton Stove Top Grill™, many of the recipes in this book are adaptable for outdoor grills or for indoor broiling.

Printed and bound in the USA
Published by 101 Productions/The Cole Group
4415 Sonoma Highway
PO Box 4089
Santa Rosa, CA 95402-4089

1 2 3 4 5 6 7 8 9
91 92 93 94 95 96

Library of Congress Catalog Card Number in process
ISBN 1-56426-505-4

My thanks to Sandi Bradley, Rob Humrickhouse, and David Marion for their help in making this book possible.

Table of Contents

The Stovetop Grill

Enjoying the unique aroma and flavor of barbecued meats and other foods grilled outdoors has for generations been one of America's great summer pastimes. The advent of the "stovetop grill" now brings the benefits of outdoor barbecuing into the home kitchen, enabling cooks to grill indoors year-round, no matter what the season or climate.

Inspired in 1986 by the *bulgogi*, a cone-shaped brass grill that has been used for centuries in Asia, Max Burton and his daughter, Linda, developed the Burton Stove Top Grill™, as well as a line of accessories for indoor grilling. The Burton grill was the first specifically designed for Western stoves and ranges.

The concept of indoor grilling provides an amazing degree of versatility. In addition to expanding the "barbecuing" season, this cooking technique makes it possible to grill virtually anything indoors: meat, fish, and poultry; vegetables; and even fruits and desserts. The recent development of a double-burner grill makes it feasible to grill complete meals. The larger grill accommodates both a greater volume and variety of foods, from appetizers to desserts. And, since the larger grill covers two stove burners, the potential to select different cooking temperatures for each side of the grill provides even greater culinary versatility.

The menus in this book were developed using the Burton Stove Top Grill™. However, they can be prepared using other indoor grills or easily adapted for outdoor barbecues. Regardless of the type of grill used, the recipes in *Grill It In! Recipes for the Stovetop Grill* provide delicious, healthful alternatives to fried foods, an important benefit in light of the growing health concerns over fat consumption and cholesterol.

Barbara Grunes

Well over two million Americans now cook with the more than two dozen cookbooks written by Barbara Grunes. Featuring recipes and techniques from international and regional cuisines, some of her more popular titles include *Poultry On The Grill, Soups and Stews, Lunch & Brunch, Ultimate Food Processor Cookbook, Mexican Cookbook,* and the highly regarded *Fish On The Grill,* which has sold more than 450,000 copies.

Barbara has successfully drawn upon her experience as a mother of five and her extensive background in the culinary arts, where she has both taught cooking classes and consulted on matters of cuisine, to develop recipes and methods based on a practical and simplified approach to cooking. Without sacrificing elegance, authenticity, or an appreciation for the new and unusual, Barbara's books provide the home chef with a wide range of tantalizing meals and menus.

After several years as a food columnist for the *Chicago Sun Times,* Barbara is currently a contributor for a number of national and local periodicals. She and her husband reside in the Chicago area, where her children often return to sample her latest recipes.

Introduction

The stovetop grill has become indispensable to me during the time I have been developing and testing the recipes for this book. I'm sure that once you discover how versatile and fun grilling indoors can be, the stovetop grill will become a permanent fixture atop your kitchen range, as it is on mine.

Although I created the recipes for this book using the Burton Stove Top Grill™, all types of indoor grills give the home chef the potential to achieve the delicious, healthful results unique to grilled foods.

Magnificent flavor is only one of several benefits of preparing and serving foods hot from the stovetop grill. A primary goal in writing this cookbook has been to demonstrate the nutritional benefits of grilling as a delicious alternative to frying and sautéing. Proper grilling significantly reduces the fat content of many foods, an important consideration in these times of heightened awareness regarding health concerns.

Vegetables and other foods prepared on the indoor grill cook quickly and retain the color and crunchy texture that are so often lost in outdoor grilling, steaming, and other cooking methods. The steam generated in the drip pan keeps grilled food tender and juicy on the inside, while the high heat of the grill surface sears the outside quickly and beautifully.

Perhaps the greatest advantage of stovetop grilling is its incredible simplicity, convenience, and versatility. Compared to other cooking methods, preparation and cooking time are vastly minimized, and clean-up is a dream. After allowing the grill and drip pan to cool, you simply wash both with warm, soapy water. Both the grill and drip pan are dishwasher-safe.

Using your indoor grill enlivens any meal, whether you are cooking for family or a group of friends. Grilled appetizers make a splendid addition to an early evening gathering, a cocktail party, or an afternoon or evening viewing of a sports telecast. Consider arranging a variety of meats, vegetables, and accompaniments on trays and encouraging your guests to grill their own selections.

Included are two dinner suggestions that are as fun to prepare as they are enjoyable to eat. The Dim Sum Brunch makes an unusual and exciting party menu, and the Tableside Sukiyaki dinner is a simple-to-make feast that surely will be appreciated from beginning to end.

Using a Stovetop Grill

To begin, always fill the reservoir of the drip pan with water and refill as necessary, occasionally pouring in a bit of water on the edge of the drip pan. Do not pour water directly on the grill surface, since doing so will reduce the heat.

Preheating the grill is very important. The grill surface must be hot. Not all grills are designed to take high heat, so *always* follow the manufacturer's recommendations.

Once you have seared both sides of a cut of meat, poultry, or fish, you can turn down the heat on the stove to medium. The meat should be very juicy and tender when removed from the grill. Always avoid overcooking.

Cooking times will definitely vary, depending on the type and thickness of the food being grilled. While the no-stick coating makes oiling the grill surface unnecessary, you can use a light coating of vegetable oil or cooking spray, if desired.

Suggestions . . . Dos and Don'ts

Use the entire grill surface. You are certainly not limited to the non-slotted area of the grill surface. In fact, the moisture rising through the slots greatly enhances the cooking process, so feel free to frequently move foods around on the surface during grilling.

Adding herbs and spices to the water in the drip pan before grilling can add subtle flavors to a variety of dishes. Use your own judgment and imagination as you experiment. You can also add red or white wines, beer, or fruit juices to the water.

A small amount of liquid smoke flavoring in the water can provide a subtle taste addition. For an authentic outdoor flavor, you can sprinkle the liquid smoke flavoring directly on meats as they are grilling.

I do recommend marinades and have included them in many recipes. Marinating adds flavor and tenderizes the food.
For kabobs and brochettes, I recommend the use of wooden skewers, which should be soaked in water before using on the grill to prevent burning.

After you have used your grill, always allow it to cool completely before moving it from the stove. Always use caution in transferring the drip pan from stove to sink.

Almost all recipes or favorite dishes that you have prepared on your outside grill can easily be adapted for indoor grilling; bad weather will no longer limit your ability to enjoy grilled meals.

APPETIZERS

■ Appetizers excite the appetite and prepare the palate for the subsequent courses of a meal. As finger food or hors d'oeuvres appetizers heighten camaraderie among diners and are an attractive and scrumptious addition to entertaining.

■ I feel that appetizers too often are considered "company-only" food. In fact, an occasional hot appetizer will not only spice up a routine family meal, but will also serve as a delightful taste complement or contrast to the evening entrée.

■ Whether you are preparing for a formal dinner party or a cocktail party, or merely adding zest to a family dinner, the grill is perfectly designed for producing "sure-hit" hot appetizers.

Dim Sum Brunch

Stuffed Shiitake Mushrooms
Stuffed Sweet Peppers
Noodles with Chinese Barbecued Pork
Rumaki with Pineapple Sauce
Gingered Papaya

Dim Sum means "something to dot the heart with." The concept of serving a group of many small dishes began in the tea houses of Canton. This wonderful array of dishes is usually served around lunchtime.

The barbecued pork, stuffed mushrooms, and stuffed peppers can be prepared ahead, frozen and reheated at serving time. For an authentic atmosphere, use chopsticks.

Ingredients, including sesame oil, chili paste, shiitake mushrooms, snow peas, and Chinese five-spice powder can be purchased at most supermarkets or at specialty food stores.

Serves 8 to 10

Stuffed Shiitake Mushrooms

18 to 20 large dried shiitake mushrooms, washed, stems removed
1/2 cup dry sherry

■ Filling

1/4 pound lean pork, cut in 3/4-inch cubes
1/4 pound uncooked shrimp, washed, deveined, patted dry
6 water chestnuts
1 egg white
1 tablespoon cornstarch

■ Sauce

3 green onions, minced
6 tablespoons soy sauce
2 tablespoons dry sherry

Peanut oil, for brushing grill

Shiitake is the Japanese name for a mushroom that is available either fresh or dried in most specialty food stores or large supermarkets. The flavor is full-bodied and heady. Dried shiitakes, which are used in the following recipe, must be reconstituted by soaking them in water.

Cover mushrooms with hot water in a large bowl. Mix in sherry. Soak mushrooms for 1 hour at room temperature. Drain and squeeze mushrooms dry. Set aside.

To make filling, chop pork, shrimp, and water chestnuts with egg white and cornstarch in food processor fitted with steel blade.

Stuff mushroom caps with pork mixture.

To make sauce, mix onions, soy sauce, and sherry in small saucepan. Cook sauce over medium heat until warm, stirring often. Remove from heat.

Preheat stovetop grill. Brush grill surface lightly with oil.

Cook stuffed mushrooms, meat side down, over medium heat approximately 2 minutes. Turn mushrooms over and grill about 1 minute. Meat should be moist yet crusty. Remove to serving dish and drizzle with sauce. Serve hot.

Makes 8 to 10 servings

Stuffed Sweet Peppers

3 large red or green bell peppers

■ **Filling**

6 ounces ground pork
1 green onion, minced
1/2 teaspoon powdered ginger
2 tablespoons minced water chestnuts
2 tablespoons dry sherry
1 1/2 tablespoons soy sauce
1/4 teaspoon salt

4 tablespoons cornstarch

■ **Sauce**

3 tablespoons soy sauce
1/2 cup water
1 teaspoon sugar

Peanut oil, for brushing grill

Quarter bell peppers lengthwise by cutting along natural ridges. Remove and discard seeds.

To make filling, mix together pork, onion, ginger, water chestnuts, sherry, soy sauce, and salt in a bowl. Set aside. For easy preparation, these ingredients can be minced together in a food processor fitted with a steel blade.

Stuff pepper pieces with pork mixture. Spread cornstarch in a flat dish and press stuffed side of peppers into cornstarch. Tap off excess cornstarch. Place on dish and set aside.

Prepare sauce by combining soy sauce, water, and sugar in small saucepan. Cook over medium heat until sauce is heated, about 3 minutes. Reserve.

Preheat stovetop grill. Brush grill surface lightly with oil. Grill peppers, stuffed side down, for 1 to 2 minutes, or until stuffing is cooked on the inside and crisp on the outside. Turn peppers over and grill about 1 minute to cook pepper.

Remove stuffed peppers to serving dish and drizzle with sauce. Serve hot.

Makes 12 stuffed pepper pieces

Chinese Barbecued Pork

1 pound boneless pork loin, partially frozen

■ **Five-Spice Marinade**

2 tablespoons sugar
1/4 teaspoon salt
2 cloves garlic, minced
1 teaspoon Chinese five-spice powder
1/4 cup soy sauce
1/4 cup hoisin sauce
1/4 cup sake or dry white wine

■ **Topping**

1 tablespoon soy sauce
4 tablespoons honey
1/2 teaspoon sesame oil

Peanut oil, for brushing grill

The word hoisin *in Chinese means literally "sea-freshness sauce," although the sauce is actually wheat- or soybean-based.*

This barbecued pork can be used as an appetizer or main dish. The recipe freezes well. Make it ahead of time and defrost as needed.

Slice pork into thin strips. Combine marinade ingredients in a small bowl. Pour the marinade into a large resealable plastic bag. Add pork strips, seal bag securely, and turn it several times to coat pork. Refrigerate and marinate for 4 to 6 hours, turning occasionally. Drain pork and discard marinade.

Combine topping ingredients in a small bowl.

Preheat stovetop grill. Brush grill surface lightly with oil.

Cook pork in a single layer over high heat, turning as it cooks. Grill approximately 2 to 3 minutes. Pork should be cooked through but not overcooked. Remove pork to plate and cool. If not serving immediately, spoon barbecued pork into plastic bags, seal, and freeze until needed.

Makes 5 to 6 small servings

Noodles with Chinese Barbecued Pork

*14 ounces soft noodles
or pasta, cooked
according to package
directions*
5 green onions, minced
*1/2 pound fresh bean
sprouts, washed with
hot water and
drained*
*1/2 pound heated
barbecued pork slices
(see preceding
recipe)*
*1 cup snow peas,
trimmed*

■ Sauce

5 tablespoons soy sauce
*1 teaspoon dark brown
sugar*
1/2 teaspoon salt
2 tablespoons dry sherry
1 teaspoon sesame oil

Place cooked noodles in deep bowl. Cut noodles with kitchen scissors into 3-inch pieces. Mix in onions, bean sprouts, pork, and snow peas.

Combine sauce ingredients in a bowl. Toss noodles with sauce. Serve hot or at room temperature.

Makes 5 to 6 servings

Rumaki Brushed with Pineapple Sauce

■ Pineapple Sauce

1/2 cup sugar
1/2 cup cider vinegar
2 teaspoons soy sauce
1/4 cup pineapple juice
4 tablespoons catsup

8 chicken livers, cut in
   half, gristle discarded
8 water chestnuts,
   drained, cut in half
4 slices lean bacon, cut
   in half crosswise

8 small bamboo skewers
   or toothpicks, soaked
   in water 10 minutes,
   drained

The sauce in this recipe is a combination of pineapple juice and soy sauce. It makes a classic brushing sauce for grilled foods.

Combine sauce ingredients in small saucepan. Bring mixture to a boil over medium heat. Reduce heat to simmer and continue cooking 3 minutes, stirring often. Cool.

To prepare rumaki, arrange each liver half atop a water chestnut piece. Wrap strip of bacon around the liver and chestnut. Skewer with a toothpick or a bamboo skewer. Brush rumaki with pineapple brushing sauce.

Preheat stovetop grill. Cook rumaki over medium-high heat until liver is cooked and bacon crisp, turning 2 or 3 times and brushing rumaki with sauce during turning. Remove rumaki from grill and arrange decoratively on serving dish. Good with grilled green onion strips.

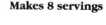

Makes 8 servings

Gingered Papaya

3 papayas, ripe but firm
2 teaspoons grated fresh ginger
1/8 teaspoon grated nutmeg
2 tablespoons freshly squeezed lime juice
1/4 cup butter or margarine, melted
3 lettuce leaves
1 lime, thinly sliced, for garnish

Ginger is a root with a highly aromatic fragrance and a sharp, pungent flavor. Fresh ginger, which can now be found in most supermarkets, is a mainstay of Chinese cooking.

Fresh ginger should be rock-hard with a smooth skin. Ginger should be stored in a cool, dry place. Peel the ginger root before grating on a fine grater. The ceramic grater I purchased in a specialty food store is inexpensive and works well.

Peel, seed, and slice papayas into 1/2-inch pieces.

Mix ginger, nutmeg, and lime juice into the melted butter. Brush papaya slices with butter mixture.

Preheat stovetop grill. Cook papaya over medium heat for 30 to 45 seconds on each side. Papaya will be warm but still firm. Brush with melted butter as you turn papaya.

To serve, arrange warm papaya slices on lettuce leaves and garnish with lime slices.

Makes 8 servings

Maryland Crab Cakes

■ Tartar Sauce

(Makes 1 1/4 cup sauce)
1 cup mayonnaise
1 small red onion,
*   minced*
1 1/2 tablespoon each:
*   chopped sweet pickles*
*   and drained capers*

■ Crab Cakes

6 ounces lump crabmeat,
*   fresh or frozen*
*   (defrosted)*
1 tablespoon minced
*   parsley*
1/4 cup mayonnaise
1/4 teaspoon each: salt
*   and white pepper*
1/2 teaspoon each: dry
*   mustard and*
*   Worcestershire sauce*
1 cup fine bread crumbs

Butter or margarine,
*   melted, to brush grill*

Lump crabmeat, used in this recipe, can be either fresh or frozen. Fresh crab, however, has a sweeter taste.
This recipe can be doubled if you are expecting additional guests.

To make sauce, blend all ingredients in a bowl. Cover and refrigerate sauce until ready to serve. Stir sauce before serving.

To make crab cakes, pick over crabmeat, discarding any gristle.

Mix together crabmeat, parsley, mayonnaise, salt, pepper, mustard, and Worcestershire sauce in a bowl. Form into crab cakes.

Spread bread crumbs on a flat dish. Lightly bread crab cakes. Set crab cakes on a dish and refrigerate before cooking.

Preheat stovetop grill. Brush grill surface with melted butter. Grill crab cakes over medium heat, turning once during grilling.

Crab cakes will be lightly browned on the outside and cooked on the inside. Remove crab cakes from the grill and place 1 cake on each dish. Serve with tartar sauce. Crab cakes are also good with garlic-flavored mayonnaise mixed with low-fat, plain yogurt.

Makes 4 servings (1 crab cake per person)

Skewered Steak Strips
with Oyster/Garlic Brushing Sauce

**1 pound flank steak,
partially frozen**

■ **Sauce**

**2 green onions, minced
1/4 cup soy sauce
1/4 cup chicken stock
1/4 cup dark brown
   sugar, firmly packed
1 teaspoon powdered
   ginger
2 cloves garlic, minced
3 tablespoons oyster
   sauce, available at
   specialty food stores
1 1/2 tablespoons dark
   molasses
1 tablespoon dry white
   wine
1 tablespoon cornstarch,
   blended with 1 table-
   spoon cold water**

**24 8-inch skewers,
   soaked in water 10
   minutes, drained
Kiwi fruit slices, for
   garnish**

Meat for kabobs, strips, or Asian dishes should be partially frozen to facilitate slicing. Slice across the grain.

Slice partially frozen meat diagonally, across the grain, into 1-inch strips.

To prepare sauce, heat all sauce ingredients, except cornstarch mixture, in a saucepan. Heat sauce to a boil over medium heat, stirring often. Reduce heat and allow mixture to simmer. Continue cooking until ingredients are well-blended for about 3 minutes. Stir in cornstarch mixture, stirring and cooking until sauce thickens slightly. Cool.

To make steak strips, thread meat onto skewers, in and out, until the meat is secure. Brush skewered steak with sauce.

Preheat stovetop grill. Cook skewered steak over medium-high heat, turning as needed. Brush meat with sauce as you turn it. Cook to taste. Meat will be browned on the outside. Remove meat from grill. Skewered steak can be kept warm in a 250° F oven. Serve hot. Good with extra sauce for dipping. Garnish with kiwi fruit slices.

Makes 24 pieces (2 to 3 pieces per person)

Chicken Livers with Grilled Figs

1 1/2 pounds chicken
   livers
3 tablespoons butter or
   margarine
1/2 teaspoon dried sage
1/4 teaspoon each: salt,
   pepper, and dried
   oregano
1/4 small onion, sliced
2 teaspoons dry sherry
3 tablespoons minced
   parsley

This dish works well as either an appetizer or as a tasty lunch. Serve with sherry and either grapes or a mixed green salad.

Cut chicken livers in half, and discard gristle.

Melt butter. Stir in sage, salt, pepper, and oregano. Set aside.

Preheat stovetop grill. Cook onions and livers over medium heat or until livers are browned, but still slightly pink inside (about 1 to 2 minutes). Do not overcook livers. Brush with seasoned butter as they grill. Place cooked livers and onions in serving bowl. Sprinkle with sherry and parsley. Serve with toothpicks, whole wheat toast triangles, and grilled figs (recipe follows).

Makes 8 servings

Grilled Figs

8 ripe fresh figs, cut in
   half
2 tablespoons butter or
   margarine, melted
2 tablespoons light
   brown sugar

Figs have a lusciously soft, sweet flavor. If fresh figs are unavailable, dried figs can be used, but they must be reconstituted by soaking them in warm water for 20 minutes.

Brush cut side of figs with butter and sprinkle with sugar.

Preheat stovetop grill. Brush grill surface with butter. Grill figs, cut side down, over medium heat, until golden brown (about 1 1/2 minutes). Watch that sugar doesn't burn. Grill only until sugar melts and figs are warm.

Remove figs from grill and place cut side up around chicken livers.

Miniature Burgers

**2 pounds ground chuck
  steak
1 onion, minced
1 teaspoon
  Worcestershire sauce
1/2 teaspoon each: salt,
  garlic powder, and
  dry mustard
1/4 teaspoon pepper
1 egg (or 2 egg whites)**

**Extra virgin olive oil, for
  brushing grill**

These miniature burgers are especially popular for children's parties or watching sports telecasts.
For best results, grind your own beef or choose your meat and ask the butcher to custom grind it for you.

Combine all ingredients except oil. Shape into 16 miniature hamburger patties. Set patties on dish and refrigerate until grilling time.

Preheat stovetop grill. Brush grill surface lightly with oil. Cook hamburger patties to taste over high heat. Burgers will be crusty on the outside. Turn once or twice during cooking. Remove burgers and place on warm whole wheat rolls.

Serve burgers with chips, pickles, lettuce, tomato slices, relish, mustard, and catsup.

Makes 8 servings (16 burgers)

English Muffin Pizzas

*Extra virgin olive oil, for
  brushing grill*
3 English muffins, split
*6 thin slices mozzarella
  cheese (cut to fit
  English muffins)*
*6 tablespoons tomato
  sauce or catsup*
*Oregano, garlic powder,
  and pepper or hot-
  pepper flakes, to taste*

These miniature pizzas make a fun lunch for children or a filling appetizer for adults. Be creative and add your favorite toppings such as chopped green bell pepper, sliced mushrooms, anchovy strips, or chopped onion. Or provide small bowls of the toppings and let your guests sprinkle their own choice of toppings over the muffin pizzas.

Preheat stovetop grill. Brush grill surface lightly with oil. Cook English muffins, cut side down, over medium-high heat, pressing down with a spatula, about 1 minute. Turn muffins over. Place a slice of cheese on top of each muffin. Grill about 1 minute. The muffin will have golden brown areas on both top and bottom. Cheese will begin to melt along edges.

Remove muffins from grill and set on a dish. Place 1 tablespoon tomato sauce on center of each muffin. Spread sauce to cover most of top of muffin, using the back of a teaspoon. Sprinkle muffin with oregano, garlic powder, and pepper to taste. Serve muffins hot.

Makes 6 servings

Breakfast English Muffin with Canadian Bacon

Extra virgin olive oil, for brushing grill
3 English muffins, split
6 slices Canadian bacon
1 tomato, cut into 6 thin slices
1 onion, cut into 6 thin rounds
Dried basil, to taste

Preheat stovetop grill. Brush grill surface lightly with oil. Cook English muffins, cut side down, over medium-high heat, pressing down with a spatula, about 1 minute. Turn muffins over. Place a slice of cheese on top of each muffin. Grill about 1 minute. The muffin will have golden brown areas on both top and bottom. Remove muffins to serving plate. Grill bacon until cooked to taste (about 1 minute on each side). Place bacon atop each muffin.

Set a tomato slice over bacon. Grill onion about 30 seconds on each side. Onion will char slightly. Place onion on top of tomato. Sprinkle with basil. Serve immediately.

Makes 6 servings

Beef Roll-Arounds

■ *Honey Brushing Sauce*

3 tablespoons soy sauce
2 tablespoons honey
2 tablespoons dry white wine
2 tablespoons oyster sauce
1/4 teaspoon each powdered garlic and Chinese five-spice powder

1/2 pound beef tenderloin
3 stalks celery

Chinese ingredients are available at large supermarkets or in specialty food stores.

Mix the sauce ingredients together in a bowl. Set aside.

Chill meat. Cut into 18 thin slices. Press meat slices with a spatula.

Cut celery stalks in half horizontally. Then cut celery again into 3-inch pieces, making eighteen 3-inch stalks. Roll a piece of meat around each celery stalk. Brush beef roll-arounds with sauce.

Preheat stovetop grill. Grill beef roll-arounds, seam side down, over medium-high heat. Turn roll-arounds as they cook, brushing with sauce during turning. Meat is done when pinkness is gone.

Remove to serving dish. Serve hot. Good with cooked noodles or fried rice.

Makes 6 servings

Grilled Shrimp Sushi

12 extra-large shrimp

1/2 pound short grain rice, washed, drained well

1 tablespoon dry white wine

2 tablespoons rice vinegar

2 teaspoons sugar

1/2 teaspoon salt

2 teaspoons lightly toasted sesame seeds

Pickled ginger

Sushi *means rice flavored with vinegar.*

Devein and butterfly shrimp, then wash and pat dry.

Put rice in saucepan, cover with water. Bring to a boil, reduce heat to simmer, cover, and continue cooking for 15 minutes.

Meanwhile, heat wine, vinegar, sugar, and salt in small pan. Bring to a boil. Remove from heat and allow to cool.

When rice is cooked, remove from heat and let cool for 15 minutes. Spoon rice into a bowl, sprinkle with vinegar mixture, and mix well.

Form rice into oval patties the size of the shrimp and set on a platter.

Preheat stovetop grill. Grill shrimp cut side down over medium-high heat. Turn shrimp over and grill only until done. Do not overcook. Shrimp is done when it turns opaque.

To assemble sushi, place a shrimp on each rice patty and sprinkle with sesame seeds. Serve at room temperature with pickled ginger.

Makes 6 servings

Chili Sea Scallop Kabobs

■ Sauce

2 tablespoons peanut oil
1 medium onion, minced
1/2 teaspoon each:
  powdered ginger,
  minced garlic, and
  hot-pepper flakes
1/4 cup soy sauce
3 tablespoons light
  brown sugar
3 tablespoons chili paste
  with garlic (or substi-
  tute catsup)
3 tablespoons red wine
  vinegar

12 sea scallops
24 snow peas, trimmed
6 1/2 8-inch bamboo
  skewers, soaked in
  water 10 minutes,
  drained

Peanut oil, for brushing
  grill

These succulent, spicy appetizers are prepared using chili paste with garlic, which is available in specialty food stores.

To prepare sauce, heat oil in a pan. Sauté onion with ginger, garlic, and hot-pepper flakes for 2 minutes, stirring often. Add remaining sauce ingredients. Simmer 1 minute to combine ingredients.

Thread scallops and snow peas alternately onto skewers. Brush with sauce.

Preheat stovetop grill. Brush grill surface with oil. Grill kabobs over medium heat, turning once or twice during grilling or as needed. Kabobs should be cooked through, but not overcooked. Scallops will become firm and opaque. Remove kabobs from grill and serve. Good with hot white rice or fried rice.

Makes 6 servings

Szechwan Chicken Wings

2 pounds chicken wings

■ **Sauce**

1/2 cup soy sauce
3 tablespoons apricot jam
1/4 cup dry white wine
2 green onions, minced
1/2 teaspoon grated ginger
2 cloves garlic, minced
1/3 cup firmly packed dark brown sugar
2 teaspoons chili paste with garlic, available at specialty food stores, or substitute catsup
1/8 teaspoon hot-pepper flakes

Peanut oil, for brushing grill and green onions

16 green onions, trimmed

Szechwan, a province in central China, is famous for pandas and hot peppers. The cuisine of Szechwan is fast becoming one of the most popular Chinese cooking styles in the Western world.

Remove tips from chicken wings. Cut wings in half at joint. Wash wings and pat dry.

Combine sauce ingredients in a bowl. Brush wing pieces with sauce.

Preheat stovetop grill. Brush grill surface lightly with oil and cook wing pieces at medium-high heat until done. Wings will brown on the outside and be cooked on the inside. Chicken is done when it is slightly firm to the touch and juices run clear if chicken is cut with a knife. Turn wings several times during grilling and brush wings with sauce as you turn them. Remove wings to serving platter. Serve hot.

Brush onions lightly with oil. Cook onions on preheated grill over medium-high heat, turning onions once during grilling. Cook about 1 minute on each side. Serve onions hot with chicken wings.

Makes 8 servings

Anchovy Toast

16 thin slices day-old
  white bread, crusts
  removed
16 thin slices mozzarella
  cheese
2 cans (2 oz each)
  anchovy fillets,
  drained
1/2 teaspoon each:
  garlic powder and
  dried basil
Butter or margarine, for
  brushing grill

Anchovies are small, silvery fish that are generally sold as canned fillets packed in oil. They have a distinctive, highly salty flavor and are widely used as a garnish with other foods.

Cut each slice of bread in half. Place 1 slice of cheese on each of 16 pieces. Set 2 anchovy fillets on top of cheese and sprinkle with small amount of garlic and basil. Make a sandwich, covering the anchovy with another slice of bread; press the sandwich together.

Preheat stovetop grill. Brush grill surface with butter. Cook sandwiches over medium-high heat until golden brown (about 1 minute per side). Press sandwich together gently with spatula. Remove anchovy toast to plate. Serve hot. Good with antipasto, tossed salad, or tomato wedges.

Makes 8 servings

Salami/Pineapple Brochettes

■ Sauce

4 tablespoons soy sauce
2 1/2 tablespoons dark brown sugar
2 tablespoons red wine vinegar

24 pieces pineapple chunks, drained
24 1/2-inch chunks of salami
12 strips red or green bell pepper

12 small bamboo skewers or toothpicks, soaked in water 10 minutes, drained

This quick recipe is perfect for unexpected company. Salami, pineapple, and red peppers make an interesting, savory combination of tastes.

Combine sauce ingredients in a bowl. If you like, you can substitute bottled chutney for brushing sauce.

Prepare brochettes by threading 1 piece pineapple, 1 piece salami, 1 piece pineapple, 1 piece salami, and then a pepper strip, to create 12 brochettes.

Preheat grill. Cook brochettes over medium-high heat until done to taste. Turn 2 to 3 times and brush with sauce as you turn. Salami will brown slightly. Remove brochettes to serving dish. Serve hot.

Makes 6 servings (12 small brochettes)

Pork Saté with Ginger Marinade

**2 pounds pork tender-
loin, sliced about 3/4
inch thick**

■ *Ginger Marinade*

**4 green onions, minced
2 1/2 teaspoons freshly
grated ginger root
2 cloves garlic, minced
3 tablespoons freshly
squeezed lime juice
1/2 teaspoon salt
1/4 teaspoon each: hot-
pepper flakes (or to
taste) and ground
cumin
4 tablespoons water**

**24 8-inch bamboo
skewers, soaked in
water 10 minutes,
drained**

Saté *is an Indonesian appetizer of skewered, grilled
cubed meat.*

Cut pork into 1/2-inch pieces.

Combine marinade ingredients and pour into a large resealable
plastic bag. Add meat and seal bag securely closed. Turn bag
several times to coat meat. Refrigerate and marinate for 2 to 3
hours, turning occasionally. Drain meat and discard marinade.

Thread pork chunks onto skewers. Preheat stovetop grill. Grill
saté over medium-high heat until pork is slightly charred on the
outside and all traces of pink are gone. Turn often, grilling all
sides of pork. Remove saté from grill and arrange on a serving
dish. Serve saté hot with Chunky Peanut Sauce (recipe follows).

Makes 24 saté (about 8 to 10 servings)

Chunky Peanut Sauce

2 tablespoons peanut oil
3 green onions, minced
2 cloves garlic, minced
1/8 teaspoon hot-pepper
  flakes, or to taste
1 3/4 cups strong
  chicken stock
3/4 cup roughly
  chopped peanuts
1 tablespoon freshly
  squeezed lime juice
2 tablespoons dark
  brown sugar
2 tablespoons minced
  cilantro, or to taste

To prepare chunky peanut sauce, heat oil in saucepan. Sauté onions, garlic, and hot-pepper flakes for 2 minutes, stirring often. Mix in stock, peanuts, lime juice, sugar, and cilantro. Simmer for 5 to 6 minutes, stirring often. If sauce cools and thickens, add hot water, 2 tablespoons at a time, until mixture reaches desired thickness. Serve sauce hot.

Makes 1 1/2 cups

Rosemary Lamb Ribs

3 1/2 to 4 pounds lamb ribs

■ **Rosemary Marinade**

1 teaspoon dried rosemary
1/2 teaspoon each: salt and freshly ground black pepper
1 1/2 cups catsup
3 cloves garlic, minced
1 small onion, minced
3/4 cup grape jelly, heated with 2 tablespoons water
1 teaspoon Worcestershire sauce
1 tablespoon red wine vinegar

2 tablespoons dried rosemary

Rosemary is a very pungent herb. It grows in a pot in my kitchen all year around, and I clip some off whenever I need it. This handsome herb makes a pretty centerpiece or garnish as well as a tasty flavoring for meats and wild game. Sprinkle rosemary on the water in the grill pan for extra flavoring.

Remove all visible fat from lamb and cut into 2-rib sections.

Combine rosemary marinade ingredients. Pour marinade into 2 large resealable plastic bags. Divide ribs between the 2 bags and seal. Turn bags several times to coat meat. Refrigerate and marinate for 3 to 4 hours, turning occasionally. Drain the meat and reserve marinade.

Preheat grill. Sprinkle rosemary into the water in the drip pan. Replace grill surface. Grill ribs over medium-high heat, turning as needed. Ribs should be crisp on the outside and cooked on the inside. Brush with marinade as you turn ribs.

Remove ribs from grill and serve hot. Good with eggplant relish (recipe follows) and a Greek salad.

Makes 4 to 5 servings

Eggplant Relish

1 eggplant
3 tablespoons extra
   virgin olive oil

1 onion, minced
5 stalks celery, chopped
1 cup chopped mush-
   rooms
1 large tomato, chopped
2 tablespoons freshly
   squeezed lemon juice
1/3 cup tomato juice
3 tablespoons catsup
3/4 teaspoon each: dried
   oregano and dried
   basil
1/2 teaspoon each: salt
   and freshly ground
   black pepper

This spicy relish is excellent spread on white-flour crackers (thin flour wafers). Eggplant relish is also superb with raw vegetable pieces.

Peel eggplant and cut into 1/2-inch slices. Discard end pieces.

Brush eggplant slices lightly with olive oil.

Preheat stovetop grill. Cook eggplant over medium-high heat until tender. Eggplant will brown outside and be tender inside. Remove eggplant from grill and mash in a bowl.

Combine remaining ingredients and mix well. Taste and adjust seasonings.

Cover eggplant relish and refrigerate until serving time. Stir before serving.

Makes 4 to 6 servings

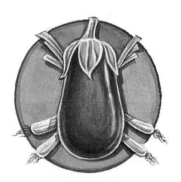

Cheese Fingers

1 pound low-fat
  mozzarella cheese
2 eggs, lightly beaten
1/4 teaspoon each: salt,
  pepper, and dried
  basil
1 1/2 cups fine white
  breadcrumbs

Cut cheese into fingers 3 inches long and 1/2 inch thick. Season beaten eggs with salt, pepper, and basil. Roll cheese fingers in bread crumbs. Coat with egg, and roll in bread crumbs once again.

Preheat stovetop grill. Grill cheese fingers over medium heat until coating is lightly browned (about 30 seconds on each side). Serve hot with cut vegetables and garlic bread.

Makes 8 servings

Cheese Coins

1/2 pound Cheddar
  cheese, shredded
3 tablespoons butter or
  margarine, at room
  temperature
3/4 cup unbleached all-
  purpose flour
1/2 teaspoon cumin
  seeds
1 teaspoon
  Worcestershire sauce
1/4 teaspoon each: salt
  and white pepper

This recipe is a favorite for cold winter afternoons. Cheese coins can be prepared ahead and frozen. Serve warm with dark bread slices and Greek olives.

Place all ingredients into a food processor fitted with steel blade. Process about 40 seconds or until all ingredients are combined.

Shape batter into 2 logs about 1 1/2 inches thick. Wrap securely in waxed paper. Chill cheese logs until firm.

At serving time, slice cheese logs into 1/4-inch rounds.

Preheat grill. Cook cheese rounds over medium heat only until warm, turning once with a spatula (about 30 seconds each side). Serve immediately.

Makes 3 dozen

Dorothy's Gyros Pita Pockets With Yogurt Cucumber Dressing

◼ Yogurt Cucumber Dressing

1 1/2 cups low-fat, plain yogurt
1/2 cup finely chopped cucumber
1/4 teaspoon each: garlic powder, salt, and white pepper

◼ Gyros

18 (or more, to taste) slices of gyros meat
6 whole wheat or plain pita bread rounds, cut in half
1 large red onion, chopped
1 large tomato, chopped

My daughter Dorothy and her friends enjoy making gyros on the stovetop grill. They cook the lamb mixture and then warm pita pockets on the grill. For gyros appetizers, cut pita bread gyros into quarters and serve with cucumber dressing. Gyros meat is available at most supermarkets.

Mix dressing ingredients in a small bowl. Cover and refrigerate until serving time.

Preheat stovetop grill. Grill gyros slices a few seconds on each side over high heat, until done to taste. Meat will brown. Remove from grill and blot off excess fat with paper toweling. Grill pita pockets a few seconds on each side, until pockets are warm. Open pocket and fill with meat and cucumber dressing. Cut each pocket in half and arrange on serving dish.

Serve with a bowl of chopped red onion and tomatoes.

Makes 6 servings

SALADS

■ While salads are not generally associated with grilling, these recipes make a splendid addition to your repertoire. Salads are traditionally perceived as an addendum to a meal, but I like to think of salad as an overture to the symphony. On the other hand, the salad can make a refreshing meal in itself—healthful, wholesome, light, and totally satisfying. Whatever your preference, the grill will help to simplify your salad preparations.

■ If the salad dish is to precede the meal, it should either complement the meal itself or it should serve to pique the palate, not, as is far too often the case, to fill the stomach.

■ I have designed these salad recipes combining hot and cold ingredients for use with the grill. Think of this as a new concept for grilling indoors. The appetites of your family and your guests will be quickened and satisfied by the salads you present to them. Grilling and salad—unique, fun, and memorable.

■ Salads make an ideal solution for many left-over dishes. Both meat and vegetables can be transformed on the grill to provide the foundation for a terrific salad.

Grilled Chicken Salad
with Pecans and Oranges

▪ Dressing

**3/4 cup low-fat, plain
  yogurt
3/4 cup mayonnaise
1/3 cup freshly
  squeezed orange juice
1 teaspoon orange zest**

▪ Salad

**1 cup chopped pecans
1 pound fettuccine
  noodles
2 skinless, boneless
  chicken breasts
1/2 teaspoon garlic
  powder
1 tablespoon extra
  virgin olive oil

1 can (6.5 oz) mandarin
  oranges, drained**

Combine dressing ingredients in a bowl. Cover and refrigerate until needed.

Spread pecans on a cookie sheet and toast in 350° F oven for about 5 to 8 minutes, stirring once. Remove nuts from oven.

Cook fettuccine in boiling water until tender or "al dente," or cook according to package directions, and drain. Place in large bowl.

Cut chicken into 1-inch strips.

Preheat stovetop grill. Mix garlic powder with oil. Brush chicken with oil and grill over medium-high heat until cooked, turning as needed and cooking 4 to 5 minutes. Chicken is done when it is slightly firm to the touch and juices run clear if chicken is cut with a knife. Remove chicken from grill. Cut into 1/2-inch cubes.

To serve, toss fettuccine and dressing. Mix in orange segments. Divide onto 4 or 5 salad plates. Place chicken and pecans on top of each salad. Serve warm or cold with grilled red onion slices.

Makes 4 servings

Italian Chicken Salad

2 skinless, boneless chicken breasts
1/4 cup extra virgin olive oil, divided

4 to 5 cups assorted greens, washed and drained
1 medium red onion, thinly sliced
2 tomatoes, sliced
1/2 cup sliced black olives

Freshly squeezed juice of 2 lemons
2 teaspoons dried oregano
1 1/2 teaspoons dried basil
2 cloves garlic, minced
1/4 teaspoon each: salt and freshly ground black pepper

2 tablespoons capers, drained
1/4 cup freshly grated Parmesan cheese

Capers are the buds of a bush native to Asia and the Mediterranean. They are pickled in vinegar brine and add a sour, pungent taste to this and other chicken, meat, and game dishes. Capers will retain their vitality as long as they remain covered by the pickling liquid in the bottle.

The strong taste of Parmesan cheese and the sharp flavor of capers give this chicken salad an interesting, refreshing quality.

Use high-quality Parmesan cheese and grate it yourself for best results.

Cut chicken into 1-inch strips.

Preheat stovetop grill. Brush grill lightly with oil and cook chicken strips over medium-high heat until done, about 5 minutes, turning as needed. Chicken is done when it is slightly firm to the touch and juices run clear when chicken is cut with a knife. Remove from grill and reserve.

Divide and arrange greens on individual salad plates. Put onions, tomatoes, olives, and chicken strips over greens.

Mix remaining oil, lemon juice, oregano, basil, garlic, salt, and pepper. Drizzle over salads. Sprinkle with capers and freshly grated Parmesan cheese. Serve quickly so the chicken is hot and the salad is cold. Great with bread sticks.

Makes 4 to 5 servings

Southwest Chicken Salad

■ Dressing

**2 cups low-fat, plain
    yogurt
2 tablespoons chili
    powder, divided
1 teaspoon ground
    cumin
1/2 cup chopped
    cilantro**

■ Chicken Salad

**1/4 cup fresh jalapeño
    peppers
2 red bell peppers,
    seeded, cut in 1/2-inch
    strips
2 skinless, boneless
    chicken breasts
1 small head lettuce,
    washed, torn into
    small pieces
1 red onion, thinly sliced
2 tomatoes, chopped
1 cup sharp longhorn
    Cheddar, shredded
1 cup tortilla chips**

**Peanut oil, for brushing
    grill
1/4 teaspoon each:
    garlic powder and
    chili powder**

Southwest cooking has become very popular. It is not only colorful, but also very zestful and tasty.

Like many Southwest recipes, this one calls for jalapeño peppers. Always use gloves when handling peppers as the oils will burn eyes or mouth on contact.

Seed, drain, and chop jalapeño peppers. Cut bell peppers into 1/2-inch strips; discard seeds.

Cut chicken into 3/4-inch pieces.

Combine dressing ingredients in bowl. Cover and refrigerate until needed.

Place lettuce in large salad bowl. Add onions, tomatoes, cheese, jalapeño peppers, and chips. Toss with dressing.

Preheat stovetop grill. Brush grill surface lightly with oil. Grill bell peppers over medium-high heat, turning frequently until softened. Remove from grill and arrange on top of salad.

Brush chicken with oil; sprinkle with garlic powder and chili powder. Grill over medium-high heat until cooked, about 5 minutes. Chicken is done when it is slightly firm to the touch and when juices run clear if chicken is cut with a knife. Remove from grill; place chicken on salads and serve.

Makes 6 to 8 servings

Cajun Turkey Salad

■ *Cajun Spice Mix*

*1 tablespoon dried
   minced onions
1 teaspoon cayenne
1/2 teaspoon each:
   garlic powder, dried
   thyme, celery salt, and
   salt*

■ *Turkey Salad*

*3 large slices white
   turkey meat
1/2 cup chopped
   walnuts
1 onion, sliced
1/4 cup low-fat, plain
   yogurt
1/4 cup mayonnaise
3 cups lettuce, shredded
   into small pieces
1 large tomato, chopped*

Combine Cajun spices.

Preheat grill. Cook turkey over medium-high heat, brushing with Cajun spice mix as you grill. Grill about 1 minute on each side. Remove turkey from grill, dice, and place in bowl. Combine walnuts, onion, yogurt, and mayonnaise and toss with turkey, lettuce, and tomato.

Serve cold or at room temperature.

Makes 4 to 6 servings

Linguine with Grilled Seafood

■ Spinach and Sherry Dressing

2 tablespoons butter or margarine
3 green onions, minced
12 ounces fresh spinach, trimmed, washed, dried
1/2 teaspoon each: salt, dried tarragon, and garlic powder
3 tablespoons dry sherry

Peanut oil, for brushing grill
3/4 pound bay scallops
12 extra-large shrimp, peeled, deveined
1/2 pound mushrooms, sliced in half

1 package (1 lb) linguine, cooked according to package directions, drained
2 to 3 tablespoons freshly grated Romano cheese

Combining scallops, shrimp, and mushrooms sprinkled with freshly grated Romano cheese, this dish can serve as a salad, a side dish, or an extremely satisfying meal in itself.

Romano cheese is a sharp and tangy, hard cheese that gives a punch to the mildly sweet taste of the shrimp and scallops used in this seafood pasta salad.

Heat butter in medium saucepan. Sauté onions until tender, about 5 minutes, stirring often. Stir in spinach, salt, tarragon, and garlic powder. Continue cooking 4 to 5 minutes, then mix in sherry. Remove from heat and set aside.

Preheat stovetop grill. Brush grill surface lightly with oil. Cook scallops and shrimp over high heat, turning occasionally. Do not overcook. Scallops and shrimp will turn opaque and will be slightly firm to the touch. Grill mushrooms one minute on each side.

Toss scallops, shrimp, and mushrooms with pasta. Mix with dressing. Sprinkle cheese on top and serve hot.

Makes 4 servings

Grilled Monkfish Salad on Hot Dog Rolls

**2 tablespoons butter or
 margarine, melted
1/4 teaspoon garlic
 powder**

1 pound monkfish

**1/2 cup mayonnaise
4 ribs celery, minced
4 green onions, minced
1/4 teaspoon each:
 garlic powder, salt,
 and cayenne
4 hot dog rolls, split**

Monkfish has a sweet, lobster-like taste. I have adapted this recipe from one I enjoyed in New England—lobster chunks on hot dog rolls. This dish makes an excellent luncheon meal.

Mix melted butter and garlic powder together in a small bowl.

Preheat stovetop grill. Brush monkfish with melted butter and grill over medium-high heat until done, for about 4 to 5 minutes, turning after 2 minutes. Brush fish with melted butter as you turn it. Monkfish will be opaque and slightly firm to the touch.

Flake grilled fish and place in a bowl. Mix in mayonnaise, celery, onions, garlic powder, salt, and cayenne.

Brush rolls with any remaining butter and heat on grill, about 30 seconds per side.

Open rolls and mound with monkfish salad. Serve with chips and butter pickles.

Makes 6 servings

Grilled Tuna Salad Mediterranean-Style

1/4 pound fresh tuna
1 tablespoon extra
    virgin olive oil
1/2 teaspoon garlic
    powder

1 cup boiled potatoes,
    diced
1 onion, chopped
1 green bell pepper
1 cup green beans,
    chopped, drained
1/2 cup mayonnaise
1/2 teaspoon each: dried
    basil, salt, and pepper

4 lettuce leaves
1 tomato, sliced, for
    garnish

Imagine the delicious taste of fresh tuna, grilled to perfection on the stovetop grill.

Cut tuna into 3/4-inch strips.

Preheat grill. Brush tuna with oil. Sprinkle tuna with garlic powder and cook over medium-high heat, 2 minutes on each side. Tuna will be firm to the touch and opaque. Do not overcook. Remove tuna to mixing bowl. Flake into small chunks. Mix in potato, onions, pepper, beans, mayonnaise, basil, salt, and pepper. Toss lightly.

Arrange lettuce leaf on each plate. Spoon tuna salad onto lettuce leaf and garnish with tomato.

Serve warm or cold with French bread.

Makes 4 servings

Seafood Spinach Pasta Salad

■ Dressing

1/2 cup extra virgin
olive oil
1/4 cup balsamic
vinegar
1/4 teaspoon each:
paprika and dried
mustard
1/2 teaspoon each:
garlic powder, salt,
and pepper
3 tablespoons chopped
chives

1 package (1 lb) spinach
pasta, cooked accord-
ing to package direc-
tions, drained
1 medium red onion,
thinly sliced
1 medium zucchini, cut
in half horizontally
3/4 pound haddock
fillets
1/2 pound sea scallops
4 tablespoons extra
virgin olive oil

1/2 pound shredded
crab meat (you may
substitute imitation
crab meat)
1 tablespoon sesame
seeds, lightly toasted
1 teaspoon dill seed

For this wonderful fish, vegetable, and pasta combination, use either leftover seafood, or, for a fresher, more elegant taste and appearance, use fresh fish.

When purchasing fresh spinach, always select crisp, dark green leaves. Avoid spinach leaves that are yellow or wilted.

To make dressing, blend oil and vinegar in a bowl. Mix in remaining dressing ingredients. Cover and refrigerate until needed. Mix before serving.

Place pasta in bowl. Toss with red onions and set aside.

Preheat grill over medium-high heat. Brush cut side of zucchini with oil. Grill 2 minutes per side; cut side of zucchini will brown slightly. Remove from grill, slice, and add to pasta dish.

Brush haddock fillets and scallops with oil. Grill haddock fillets 2 minutes per side. Fish will be opaque and flake easily. Remove to plate, flake, and add to pasta salad.

Grill scallops 2 1/2 minutes per side. Remove from grill and add to salad. Toss salad with shredded crab, sesame seeds, and dill. Add dressing to taste. Serve warm or cold.

Makes 6 to 8 servings

Grilled Flank Steak on Lettuce

1 pound flank steak
2 tablespoons peanut oil

1/2 tablespoon each:
   minced garlic and
   ground cumin

1 large onion, thinly
   sliced
2 red bell peppers,
   seeded, sliced
Juice of 2 limes
1/4 to 1/2 teaspoon hot-
   pepper flakes
2 cucumbers, peeled,
   thinly sliced
1/3 cup minced cilantro

4 large lettuce leaves

Cilantro, also called Chinese parsley, *is the leaf of the coriander plant, which is part of the carrot family. Using cilantro in cooking adds an interesting aromatic dimension to many dishes.*

Use thinly sliced flank steak for this recipe.

Cut flank steak into 1-inch strips, against the grain.

Preheat stovetop grill over medium-high heat. Brush grill surface lightly with peanut oil.

Sprinkle steak with garlic and cumin. Grill about 6 minutes, turning 2 or 3 times as needed. Meat will be browned on outside and medium-well on inside. Toss meat with remaining ingredients.

Place 1 lettuce leaf on each plate. Divide salad and spoon onto lettuce leaves. Serve immediately. Good with whole wheat rolls.

Makes 4 to 5 servings

Warm Cheese and Tomato Salad with Mustard Seed Vinaigrette

■ Mustard Seed Vinaigrette

3/4 cup extra virgin olive oil
1 clove garlic, minced
6 tablespoons tarragon vinegar
2 tablespoons freshly squeezed lemon juice
1/2 tablespoons coarse mustard
1/2 teaspoon each: salt and freshly ground black pepper

2 large tomatoes, sliced
4 green onions, minced
3 ounces goat cheese, cut into 1/2-inch pieces

The cracked mustard seeds provide a spicy but not overpowering taste. Flavored cheese, warm from the grill, is a pleasure to taste. This recipe also makes a wonderful appetizer.

Mix oil, garlic, and vinegar in bowl. Whisk in juice, mustard, salt, and pepper. Cover and refrigerate until ready to serve. Whisk before serving.

Arrange tomatoes on plate; sprinkle with onions.

Preheat stovetop grill. Place goat cheese on grill and cook over medium heat until warm but not runny. Turn once. Set cheese on tomatoes. Drizzle with vinaigrette. Serve warm.

Makes 4 servings

Grilled Pepper Salad

3 green or yellow bell peppers
1/4 cup butter or margarine, melted
1/2 teaspoon dried oregano
1/2 teaspoon each: garlic powder and thyme
1 onion, thinly sliced

You may use bell peppers, Melrose peppers, or other sweet peppers for this recipe. Using one or more spices in the water in the drip pan of your grill can add flavor to this salad.

Cut peppers into 1/2-inch strips; discard seeds.

Mix butter with oregano, garlic powder, and thyme.

Preheat stovetop grill. Cook peppers and onions over high heat, brushing with butter mixture, and turning often, until vegetables are soft. Remove to serving platter and serve hot.

Makes 4 to 6 servings

Moroccan Pasta Salad

3 red bell peppers
1 package (6 or 8 oz)
**   whole wheat pasta**
1 tomato, chopped
1 large onion, chopped
1 can (15 oz) garbanzo
**   beans, drained**
2 tablespoons peanut oil
3/4 teaspoon ground
**   cumin**
1/2 teaspoon each: salt
**   and garlic powder**
1/2 cup sliced black
**   olives**
1/2 cups low-fat, plain
**   yogurt**

Garbanzo beans, also known as chickpeas, *are widely available either canned or dried. They add a pleasant, slightly meaty flavor and texture to this salad.*

Cook pasta according to package directions, drain. Place pasta in deep bowl. Toss with tomato, onion, and beans.

Cut bell peppers into thirds; discard seeds.

Preheat grill over medium-high heat. Brush peppers lightly with oil. Grill 1/2 minutes per side. Peppers will begin to char. Slice peppers into thin strips. Add to pasta dish.

Add all remaining ingredients, except yogurt, to pasta salad.

Toss salad with yogurt. Divide salad onto serving dishes. Serve at room temperature or cold with warm pita bread.

Makes 4 serving

Asian Salad

1 slice (1/2 lb cooked weight) ham

■ **Sesame Dressing**

3 tablespoons soy sauce
2 teaspoons sugar
1/2 cup chicken stock
1/2 teaspoon sesame oil
2 tablespoons hoisin sauce
1/2 teaspoon each: garlic powder and ground ginger

1 package (12 oz) soft noodles, available at specialty food stores
1 can (8 oz) sliced water chestnuts, drained
4 green onions, minced

1 tablespoon peanut oil, for brushing grill
1/4 teaspoon minced garlic

1 cup snow peas, trimmed

Spread sesame seeds on a cookie sheet and toast until light brown, stirring frequently.

Hint: Always keep a pair of good-quality, sharp scissors solely for use in your kitchen. Scissors are an invaluable kitchen tool.

Mix dressing ingredients in small bowl. Reserve until needed.

Cook noodles in boiling, salted water only until tender (about 2 to 4 minutes). Cut into serving pieces with kitchen scissors. Drain. Place noodles in bowl. Mix in water chestnuts and green onion.

Preheat stovetop grill over medium-high heat. Brush grill surface lightly with peanut oil. Trim all fat from ham. Cut ham into 1/2-inch slices. Sprinkle ham strips with garlic powder. Grill strips 2 minutes per side or as necessary to heat ham. Remove ham strips and combine with noodles.

Brush grill surface again with peanut oil and heat snow peas, just a few seconds on each side. Toss with noodles.

Toss salad with dressing. Arrange salad on plates and serve. Best if served warm.

Makes 4 servings

Vegetarian Eggplant Salad with Herbs and Garlic

1 large eggplant
2 tablespoons salt
4 tablespoons extra
   virgin olive oil
1 onion, sliced
1 large tomato, chopped
1/2 cup green olives
1/2 teaspoon each:
   ground cumin, salt,
   and garlic powder
1/4 teaspoon pepper

Cumin is a powerful spice, widely available in both seed and ground form. Frequently used in spicy dishes, it can easily dominate other foods.

This recipe works equally well as an appetizer or as a side dish.

Cut eggplant into 1/4- to 1/2-inch slices. Sprinkle eggplant with salt. Let stand 20 minutes. Wash off salt and pat dry with paper toweling.

Preheat stovetop grill over medium heat. Brush eggplant slices with oil. Grill eggplant until slices are crunchy and golden brown outside and soft on the inside, about 2 minutes per side. Remove eggplant from grill and put in food processor fitted with steel blade. Chop.

Brush onion slices with oil and grill 1 minute per side. Mix eggplant and onion together; chop. Add tomatoes, olives, cumin, salt, garlic powder, and pepper. Mix.

Spoon onto individual salad dishes and serve warm or cold. If you refrigerate salad, stir before serving.

Makes 4 servings

Grilled Fruit Salad
with Ginger Chutney Dressing

■ **Ginger Chutney Dressing**

Homemade Ginger Chutney (recipe follows) or 1 jar (7.5 oz) prepared chutney
1/4 cup chopped candied ginger
2 cups low-fat, plain yogurt

1 cantaloupe
1 pineapple
2 bananas
2 apples
Butter or margarine, melted, for brushing fruit

2 heads Bibb lettuce, separated

1/2 cup chopped candied ginger, optional, for garnish

To prepare dressing, combine chutney, ginger, and yogurt. Cover and refrigerate until needed. Stir before serving.

Peel all fruit. Cut cantaloupe into 1-inch wedges. Cut pineapple into 1/2-inch slices. Cut bananas and apples into 1/4- to 1/2-inch slices. Discard all cores and seeds.

Arrange lettuce on plates.

Preheat grill over medium heat. Brush fruit with melted butter. Grill cantaloupe, pineapple, and apples about 1 minute on each side. Arrange on salad plate. Grill bananas about 45 seconds on each side. Add to salad plate.

Spoon dressing over fruit, garnish with candied ginger, if desired, and serve immediately. You may want to serve a scoop of pineapple or orange sherbet in the center of the salad.

Makes 4 to 5 servings

Homemade Ginger Chutney

2 cups dried pears
3 tablespoons candied
* ginger*
1 cup golden raisins
1 small lemon, sliced
* thinly*
1 cup sliced onion
1/2 cups firmly packed
* dark brown sugar*
1/2 cup red wine vinegar
3 cloves garlic, minced
1 teaspoon Dijon
* mustard*
1/2 cup tomato sauce
1/2 teaspoon each:
* ground cinnamon,*
* ground allspice, and*
* ground cloves*

Wash and chop pears.

To prepare chutney, combine all the ingredients in medium saucepan. Simmer for 20 to 25 minutes. Stir often. Mixture will be thick. Remove from stove and cool. Spoon into covered container.

Makes 3 cups

BEEF, PORK, LAMB AND VEAL

■ Most of the recipes in this chapter call for the use of a marinade, sauce, or herbs and spices. These additions are never intended to disguise or overpower the meal itself but rather to impart a new, unique, or flavorful twist to the dish. I intend these flavorings as complements to the meat itself. The marinades and sauces are light rather than overbearing.

■ In some recipes, I have suggested adding spices to the water pan of the grill. I think you will find that this adds a very satisfying and subtle flavor to the dish. Be imaginative and experiment in flavoring the water in the grill pan.

■ I have also included the recipe and directions for preparing a sukiyaki meal. Using a portable burner and stovetop grill at tableside will make the meal more authentic and add excitement and color.

Tableside Sukiyaki

6 ounces spinach
1/2 pound medium-sized
mushrooms

■ Marinade

2 cups soy sauce
1/4 cup sugar
1/2 cup sake or dry
white wine
1/4 cup beef broth

1 pound sirloin, chilled
2 packages (2 oz each)
mung bean threads
1 large onion, thinly
sliced

1 package (15 1/2 oz)
tofu

2 tablespoons peanut oil,
for brushing grill

The term sukiyaki *comes from the Japanese "suki," meaning "hoe," and "yaki," meaning "to broil." Japanese peasants are said to have used their hoes, heated over an intense fire, as a grill plate for their meals in the fields.*

The ingredients called for in this recipe are available in specialty food stores. Arrange the sliced ingredients attractively on a platter in the kitchen, then cook them at tableside as a dramatic presentation for your family or guests.

Wash and trim spinach, then blanch and drain. Wash mushrooms and cut in half. Cut tofu into 3/4-inch pieces.

Combine marinade ingredients in a bowl. Pour marinade into a large resealable plastic bag.

Slice meat against the grain into thin strips about 2 to 3 inches long. Place meat in marinade. Seal the bag securely and turn 2 or 3 times to coat the meat. Refrigerate and marinate beef 1 hour. Drain meat and reserve marinade.

Just before serving time; bring a saucepan three fourths filled with water to a boil. Add bean threads, simmer 1 minute. Drain threads and cut into 2-inch long pieces with kitchen scissors.

For tableside grilling, arrange the food in decorative rows on a tray. Place the meat, then bean threads, spinach, onion slices, mushrooms, and tofu on tray. Bring tray of food to table and have a serving bowl handy. Use a pair of chopsticks to handle the food.

Preheat stovetop grill. Cook meat quickly over high heat, turning meat with chopsticks as it cooks.

Remove meat to serving bowl. Mix in hot bean threads and spinach. Brush grill surface lightly with peanut oil and grill onion slices and mushrooms. Add onions and mushrooms to serving bowl. Sprinkle tofu over meat and vegetables.

Serve sukiyaki hot over hot white rice. Serve Grilled Pineapple for dessert (see recipe, page 176).

Makes 4 to 6 servings

Korean Beef with Sake Marinade

**1 3/4 to 2 pounds flank
 steak**

■ Sake Marinade

1/3 cup soy sauce
**1/2 cup sake or dry
 white wine**
3/4 cup water
4 green onions, minced
1 teaspoon sesame oil
**1 tablespoon sesame
 seeds**
3 tablespoons sugar

**2 to 3 tablespoons
 peanut oil**
**1/4 teaspoon garlic
 powder**

Sake, although widely considered a Japanese wine, is technically a beer made by the fermentation of rice. Its alcohol content and flat taste make it seem like a strong wine.

For best results, partially freeze meat before slicing. Slice the beef into thin 2-inch strips, cutting against the grain.

Combine all marinade ingredients in small bowl. Divide the marinade between 2 large resealable plastic bags.

Divide meat between the 2 bags. Seal the bags securely and turn them a few times to coat the meat. Refrigerate and marinate for 2 to 3 hours, turning bags occasionally. Drain meat and discard marinade.

Preheat stovetop grill. Mix peanut oil with garlic powder. Cook meat in a single layer over medium-high heat, turning often. Brush meat with flavored oil as necessary. Beef will brown and be very tender. Remove meat to serving dish. Serve with rice and Kim Chee (recipe follows).

Makes 6 servings

Kim Chee

**1 medium bok choy,
thinly sliced into
vertical pieces
2 1/2 teaspoons salt
1 large onion, thinly
sliced
1 teaspoon crushed hot-
pepper flakes
1/4 teaspoon cayenne
4 cloves garlic, minced
1 tablespoon sugar**

Arrange sliced bok choy in a deep ceramic or glass bowl. Sprinkle bok choy with salt. Cover and let stand overnight in refrigerator.

Wash and drain bok choy. Place in a clean bowl. Mix in onion, salt, hot-pepper flakes, cayenne, garlic, and sugar. Cover loosely with waxed paper. Weigh down the kim chee, using cans of food as weights. Refrigerate kim chee for 2 to 3 days before serving. Stir once a day. Keep refrigerated. Stir again before serving.

Makes 3 1/2 to 4 cups

Skewered Beef
with Sesame Marinade

▪ Sesame Marinade

1/3 cup soy sauce
2 teaspoons red vinegar
2 teaspoons Chinese
   sesame oil
2 cloves garlic, minced
1/8 teaspoon pepper
1 tablespoon lightly
   toasted sesame seeds
1/2 cup dry white wine
   or sake

1 1/4 pounds flank steak
12 6-inch bamboo
   skewers, soaked in
   water 10 minutes,
   drained
12 2-inch pieces green
   onion

Sesame seeds have a rich, nutty flavor that is heightened by toasting the seeds for 15 to 20 minutes in a medium oven, stirring occasionally until the seeds are golden colored.

Cut meat against the grain into thin slices about 2 1/2 by 1/2 inch.

Combine all marinade ingredients in a bowl and pour marinade into a large resealable plastic bag.

Add meat strips to marinade. Seal the bag securely and turn 2 or 3 times to coat the meat. Refrigerate and marinate for 2 hours, turning bag occasionally. Drain and discard marinade.

Thread meat onto skewers, using in-and-out technique. Put a green onion on the end of each skewer.

Preheat stovetop grill. Grill kabobs over medium-high heat until meat is cooked to taste, about 3 to 4 minutes. Turn occasionally during grilling.

Remove kabobs to a serving dish. Serve kabobs hot with Chinese noodles.

Makes 4 servings

Sirloin Strips
with Red Wine Marinade
Served on Sourdough Bread

Red Wine Marinade

1 1/2 cups Burgundy
  wine
3 tablespoons extra
  virgin olive oil
1/2 teaspoon each:
  garlic powder and
  dried rosemary
2 large shallots, minced
2 tablespoons minced
  parsley

1 1/4 to 1 1/2 pounds
  lean sirloin
Peanut oil, for brushing
  meat
6 slices sourdough
  bread
Dijon mustard
Dill pickles

Cut sirloin against the grain into 1- to 2-inch strips.

Combine marinade ingredients in a bowl. Divide the marinade between 2 large resealable plastic bags.

Divide the meat between the 2 bags. Seal the bags securely and turn them 2 to 3 times to coat the meat. Refrigerate and marinate for 2 to 3 hours, turning bags occasionally. Drain and discard marinade.

Preheat stovetop grill. Brush meat strips lightly with oil. Grill meat strips over medium-high heat about 3 to 4 minutes, or until done to taste. Meat will brown and be tender. Medium-rare works best with this recipe. Remove meat to serving platter. Serve on a slice of sourdough bread with mustard and pickles. Invite guests to make their own open-faced sandwiches.

Makes 6 servings

Carpaccio-Style Steak
with Mustard Mayonnaise

1 cup mayonnaise
1 tablespoon stone-
ground mustard
1/3 cup freshly grated
Parmesan cheese

4 to 5 lettuce leaves
1 large tomato, sliced

1/2 teaspoon freshly
ground black pepper
2 tablespoons extra
virgin olive oil
1 pound lean beef
tenderloin, about
3/4 inch thick, cut into
3 pieces

1/4 cup minced parsley

Carpaccio is an Italian-style dish consisting of very thinly sliced strips of high-quality beef, preferably tenderloin, served almost raw.

Partially freeze the meat and slice it very thin.

Mix mayonnaise with mustard and cheese.

Place 1 lettuce leaf on each plate. Put a dollop of mayonnaise on the side of the plate along with a slice of tomato. Set aside.

Preheat stovetop grill. Mix pepper with oil. Brush meat with oil and pepper. Sear the meat, about 45 seconds on each side, over high heat. Remove meat from grill. Meat will be charred on the outside and very rare on the inside. Slice meat very thinly.

Divide and arrange in a fan design on lettuce. Sprinkle with parsley and serve immediately. Good with dark rye bread and antipasto. This dish can be served either as a first course or as a main dish.

Makes 4 to 5 servings

Anticuchos with Tarragon Marinade

■ Tarragon Marinade

1/4 cup extra virgin
   olive oil
1 1/2 cups tarragon
   vinegar
1/2 cup water
1/2 teaspoon chili flakes
2 cloves garlic, minced
1/2 teaspoon salt
1/4 teaspoon freshly
   ground black pepper

1 1/2 to 1 3/4 pounds
   lean sirloin steak, cut
   into 1-inch cubes
6 8-inch bamboo
   skewers, soaked in
   water 10 minutes,
   drained
Extra virgin olive oil, for
   brushing meat

2 tablespoons dried
   tarragon

Anticuchos is a South American, mainly Peruvian, dish that features strips of lean sirloin marinated with tart tarragon vinegar, chili flakes, and garlic.

Combine marinade ingredients in bowl. Pour marinade into resealable plastic bag. Add meat, seal the bag securely, and turn 2 to 3 times to coat the meat. Refrigerate and marinate 3 to 4 hours, turning bag once or twice while marinating. Drain and discard marinade.

Thread meat cubes onto skewers. Brush meat with olive oil. Sprinkle dried tarragon into water in drip pan. Replace grill surface, preheat stovetop grill. Cook kabobs over medium-high heat until done to taste, about 4 to 5 minutes. Meat will brown on outside and be done to taste on inside. Turn meat as needed during grilling to brown all sides. Serve hot with grilled leeks and a bowl of olives.

Makes 6 servings

Beef Strips with Nut Sauce

▌ Nut Sauce

1 1/2 cups chopped walnuts
1/4 cup freshly squeezed lime juice
1/4 cup chicken stock
2 green onions, minced
1/4 teaspoon ground ginger
1 1/2 cups low-fat, plain yogurt

1 1/2 pounds lean sirloin
6 pineapple chunks, drained

6 10-inch bamboo skewers, soaked in water 10 minutes, drained

Cut meat into thin strips, against the grain.

Purée walnuts, lime juice, stock, onions, and ginger in food processor fitted with steel blade or use a blender. Pour sauce into bowl, reserving 1/2 cup. Mix the reserved 1/2 cup of nut sauce with yogurt in a second bowl. Cover sauces and set aside.

Thread meat strips onto skewers, using in-and-out technique. Place a pineapple chunk at the end of each skewer. Brush with nut sauce.

Preheat stovetop grill. Cook beef over medium-high heat, 2 to 4 minutes, turning skewer 2 or 3 times as needed. Meat will be browned and cooked to taste. Do not overcook meat. Remove sliced beef to serving dish.

Pass the nut sauce as a dipping sauce. Good with pilaf or fried rice.

Makes 6 servings

Warm Corned Beef on Rye

1/4 cup sauerkraut, drained
1/2 teaspoon caraway seeds
1 package (4 oz) sliced corned beef
2 slices rye bread
Stone-ground mustard
Whole dill pickles, sliced

Stir sauerkraut with caraway seeds and set aside.

Preheat stovetop grill. Place corned beef slices on grill surface in a single layer over medium heat. Heat only until meat is warm, turning as needed. Remove meat from grill.

Brush one side of a slice of rye bread with stone-ground mustard. Place corned beef over mustard. Add sauerkraut and top with remaining slice of bread. Slice sandwich in half and serve with pickles.

Makes 1 sandwich

Mexican Barbecue and Orange Salad with Jicama

1 3/4 pounds pork
     tenderloin
6 sweet peppers
1/2 teaspoon each:
     pepper, powdered
     cumin, and garlic
     powder
1 large red onion

3 tablespoons canola oil
     or peanut oil

Jicama is the root of a Mexican vine. It is similar to the potato in consistency, but has a delicious chestnut-like taste.

Cut pork into 1/2-inch slices. Seed peppers and slice into quarters. Slice onion into 6 slices.

Mix pepper, cumin, and garlic powder into the oil.

Preheat stovetop grill. Brush pork with flavored oil. Grill pork slices over medium heat, about 1 minute per side. Place pork on serving dish. All pinkness should be gone from inside of pork. Grill peppers and onion slices about 2 minutes per side, or until done to taste, brushing as you turn. Remove vegetables and arrange with pork. Serve hot with warm tortillas and Orange Salad with Jicama (recipe follows).

Makes 6 servings

Orange Salad with Jicama

1 medium head iceberg
  lettuce
4 medium oranges,
  peeled, sliced
1/2 cup sliced, pitted
  black olives
2 tomatoes, chopped

1/4 teaspoon each: salt
  and pepper
1/2 teaspoon each: dried
  basil and chopped
  mint
1/4 cup extra virgin
  olive oil
3 tablespoons red wine
  vinegar

1/2 pound jicama,
  peeled, julienned
1/2 teaspoon chili
  powder

Peanut oil, for brushing
  grill

Clean lettuce and tear into bite-sized pieces. Arrange lettuce on 6 salad plates. Arrange orange, olives, and tomatoes on lettuce.

Mix salt, pepper, basil, and mint together in a bowl with olive oil and vinegar. Drizzle dressing over salad.

Sprinkle jicama with chili powder.

Preheat stovetop grill. Brush grill surface lightly with oil. Cook jicama over medium-high heat until warm, turning as necessary.

Divide jicama and sprinkle over salads. Serve warm.

Makes 6 servings

Pork Cutlets Provençal

Provençal Sauce

2 tablespoons extra
   virgin olive oil
1 tablespoon butter or
   margarine
2 cloves garlic, minced
1 onion, thinly sliced
3 large tomatoes, peeled,
   seeded
1 cup sliced mushrooms
1/4 cup dry white wine
2 tablespoons minced
   parsley
2 tablespoons capers
2 tablespoons sliced
   olives, for garnish
1/4 teaspoon each: salt
   and dried thyme
1/8 teaspoon fresh
   ground black pepper
2 bay leaves

1 tablespoon extra
   virgin olive oil
1/2 teaspoon minced
   parsley
4 pork cutlets, about 1/2
   inch thick

Provençe is a region in the southeast of France, along the Mediterranean Sea. The cooking and tastes of this area have been strongly influenced by the Mediterranean climate and tradition. Provençal dishes tend to be heavier and heartier than those in other regions of France.

To make sauce, heat oil and butter in saucepan over medium heat. Add garlic and onion and sauté for 4 minutes. Add remaining ingredients and simmer for 3 minutes longer, stirring occasionally. Remove sauce from heat. Reheat sauce to serve.

Preheat stovetop grill. Mix olive oil with parsley and brush grill surface with flavored oil. Cook cutlets over medium-high heat until all traces of pink are gone and cutlets are browned on the outside. Turn once during grilling. Remove cutlets to individual serving dishes. Drizzle with sauce. Serve with green salad.

Makes 4 servings

Pork Chops with Cornmeal Breading

4 pork chops

■ **Breading**

1 1/2 cups cornmeal
2 tablespoons minced parsley
1/2 teaspoon each: powdered garlic and chili powder
1/4 teaspoon each hot-pepper flakes and dried onion flakes

Extra virgin olive oil, for brushing grill

This recipe is unique in that no egg is used in the breading. The chops are rolled in seasoned cornmeal, which forms a nice crust when the chops are grilled.

Serve this disk with Mango Chutney, a wonderful balance of sweet and spicy flavor that is a perfect accompaniment to this and many other meat dishes.

Mix breading ingredients and place mixture on a flat plate.

Roll pork chops in cornmeal mixture. Let chops stand for 10 minutes.

Preheat stovetop grill. Brush grill surface lightly with olive oil. Cook pork chops over medium-high heat for about 3 to 4 minutes, until all traces of pink are gone on the inside and the meat is crusty on the outside. Turn once during grilling.

Remove chops to individual plates and serve with Mango Chutney (recipe follows). Good with sliced cucumbers and tomatoes.

Makes 4 servings

No-Cook Mango Chutney

3 large ripe mangoes, peeled, chopped
1 small red onion, minced
2 teaspoons candied, minced ginger
4 1/4 cups freshly squeezed orange juice
1 1/2 tablespoons light brown sugar
1/4 teaspoon each: ground cloves and ground cinnamon
1/8 teaspoon hot-pepper flakes

Mix all ingredients and let stand 30 minutes. Cover and refrigerate until serving time. Stir and serve.

Makes about 3 cups

Barbecued Pork Chops

■ Smoky Barbecue Sauce

3 tablespoons peanut oil
1 large onion, minced
3 cloves garlic, minced
4 large tomatoes, chopped
1 can (8 oz) tomato sauce
1/2 teaspoon mesquite liquid smoke flavoring, optional
3/4 teaspoon ground cumin
1/4 teaspoon each: salt, fresh ground pepper, and hot-pepper flakes
3 tablespoons dark brown sugar
2 tablespoons cider vinegar

4 large cloves garlic, crushed
Peanut oil, for brushing grill
8 thin pork chops, about 1/2 inch thick, excess fat removed

In this recipe, use crushed garlic cloves in the water in the drip pan. Mesquite liquid-smoke flavoring lends color and a slightly smoky taste to the chops.

Garlic cloves add an aromatic touch to the pork chops.

Heat oil in saucepan. Sauté onion and garlic 4 minutes over medium heat, stirring often. Mix in remaining sauce ingredients and simmer for 10 minutes, stirring occasionally. Cool and set aside.

Put crushed garlic cloves into the water in the drip pan of the grill. Replace grill surface and preheat grill over medium-high heat. Brush grill surface lightly with oil. Grill chops about 2 to 3 minutes per side or until pork chops are done to taste and all traces of pink have disappeared. Brush chops lightly with barbecue sauce as you turn them. Pass extra sauce at the table for guests to enjoy.

Serve with warm tortillas and stewed apples.

Makes 4 servings

Mixed Grill with Thyme and Maple Glazed Onions

**4 shoulder lamb chops,
1/2 inch thick, excess
fat removed**
**3 3-ounce veal medal-
lions, cut from the loin**
**Extra virgin olive oil, for
brushing lamb and
veal**
**1 tablespoon chopped
fresh thyme leaves**
**1/4 teaspoon each: salt
and pepper**
4 sausage links
Fresh thyme for garnish

Brush the lamb and veal with oil, then sprinkle with thyme, salt, and pepper.

Preheat stovetop grill. Cook lamb, veal, and sausage links over medium-high heat, about 1 1/2 to 2 minutes per side. Turn once or twice during cooking. Brown sausage on all sides, until cooked. Test for doneness by cutting into a chop to see if it is the correct stage of doneness for your taste. Chops are best if slightly pink inside.

To serve, place 1 chop, 1 medallion, and 1 link on each plate and garnish with thyme. Serve with Maple Glazed Onions (recipe follows).

Makes 4 servings

Maple Glazed Onions

12 small boiling onions, each about 1 inch in diameter
3 tablespoons butter or margarine, cut into 1/2-inch pieces
3 tablespoons maple syrup

Preheat the oven to 400° F.

Cook onions in briskly boiling water, uncovered, for 2 minutes. Drain the onions in a sieve or a colander.

With a small, sharp knife, trim the stem ends, slip off the white, parchment-like skins, and cut the tops from the onions.

Arrange the onions in a baking dish just large enough to hold them in a single layer. Dot onions with butter. Drizzle onions with syrup. Bake 20 minutes or until onions are tender, stirring once or twice to coat onions with syrup. Onions are done when they show no resistance when pierced deeply with the point of a small knife.

Serve hot.

Makes 4 servings

Lamb Chops

1/2 teaspoon each:
  powdered garlic,
  dried thyme, and
  dried rosemary
1/4 teaspoon each: salt
  and freshly ground
  pepper
4 shoulder lamb chops,
  cut 1/2 inch thick,
  excess fat removed

Extra virgin olive oil, for
  brushing grill

Combine garlic, thyme, rosemary, salt and pepper. Rub mixture over lamb chops on both sides.

Preheat stovetop grill. Brush grill surface lightly with oil. Cook lamb chops over medium-high heat. Grill, turning once or twice until chops have browned slightly on the outside and are done to taste on the inside. I prefer lamb with just a hint of pink in the center. You may prefer chops rare or well-done.

Place a chop on each plate and serve hot.

Makes 4 servings

Lamb Chops Drizzled with Armagnac

4 shoulder lamb chops, cut 1/2 inch thick, excess fat removed
4 tablespoons freshly squeezed orange juice
1 teaspoon dried basil
1/2 teaspoon dried oregano
1/4 teaspoon pepper
1 tablespoon orange zest, for garnish

2 tablespoons Armagnac, or to taste

Armagnac is an increasingly popular, dark, rich brandy that originates in Gascony, in the southwest of France.

Set lamb chops in a shallow dish. Brush chops with orange juice and sprinkle with basil, oregano, and pepper. Let chops stand for 1 hour.

Preheat stovetop grill. Cook lamb chops over medium-high heat. Grill, turning once or twice, until chops have browned slightly on the outside and are done to taste on the inside. I prefer lamb with just a hint of pink in the center. However, you may prefer chops rare or well-done.

Place a chop on each plate and drizzle the lamb with Armagnac. Top with orange zest.

Serve hot with stewed prunes and Garlic Potatoes (see page 171).

Makes 4 servings

Crumb-Topped Lamb Chops

■ Crumb Topping

1/2 teaspoon each: dried oregano, dried thyme, dried rosemary, and salt

1/4 teaspoon fresh ground pepper

3 tablespoons extra virgin olive oil

1 tablespoon dry white wine

2 teaspoons dry mustard

1 1/2 cups fine wholewheat bread crumbs

2 1/2 tablespoons dried rosemary

2 tablespoons extra virgin olive oil, for brushing chops

6 loin lamb chops, cut 1/2 inch thick

Use a sprinkling of rosemary in the water in the drip pan of the grill with this recipe. It will serve as an aromatic and give a delicate flavoring to the meat.

Prepare topping by mixing together oregano, thyme, rosemary, salt, pepper, olive oil, wine, and mustard. Toss herb mixture with crumbs. Spread crumb topping on a flat dish and set aside.

Sprinkle 2 tablespoons rosemary into the water of the drip pan of the grill. Replace grill surface and preheat grill. Brush grill surface lightly with oil. Roll chops in crumb topping. Grill chops over medium-high heat, turning chops once. Chops will be crusty on the outside and cooked to taste on the inside. Do not overcook. Remove lamb chops and set on individual dishes. Serve hot.

Makes 6 servings

Shish Kabobs
with Shallot Sauce

■ Marinade

1/2 cup extra virgin olive
  oil
1/4 teaspoon freshly
  ground black pepper
1/4 cup balsamic vinegar
2 cloves garlic, crushed
1/2 teaspoon dried
  rosemary
1/4 teaspoon salt

■ Kabobs

1 1/2 pounds leg of lamb,
  cut into 3/4-inch cubes
4 medium onions, cut in
  quarters
16 pieces green pepper,
  cut into squares
8 cherry tomatoes

4 10-inch bamboo
  skewers, soaked in
  water for 10 minutes,
  drained

■ Shallot Sauce

3 shallots, minced
2 cloves garlic, minced
2 tablespoons butter or
  margarine
2 tablespoons dry white
  wine
1/2 cup beef stock
1/2 teaspoon dried
  rosemary

Shish kabob *is an Arabic term meaning "skewered meat."*

The marinade for this recipe is made using a balsamic vinegar—an Italian, wine-based, aged vinegar. This vinegar is mellow and sweet-and-sour, with an incredible fragrance.

Combine marinade ingredients in bowl.

Divide kabob ingredients and thread onto skewers. Arrange skewers in shallow dish. Pour the marinade over the kabobs and refrigerate for 4 to 6 hours, turning occasionally. When ready to grill, drain and discard marinade.

While kabobs are marinating, prepare Shallot Sauce. Heat butter in a frying pan. Sauté shallots and garlic for 3 minutes over medium heat. Stir in wine, stock, and rosemary. Simmer sauce for 3 minutes. Remove from heat and set aside. Reheat sauce before serving.

Preheat stovetop grill. Cook kabobs over medium-high heat, turning frequently, until lamb is brown on the outside and done to taste on the inside (about 4 to 6 minutes). Remove skewers to serving dish. Drizzle with hot shallot sauce. Serve hot with rice pilaf.

Makes 4 servings

Lemon Veal Cutlets
with Mushrooms and Shallots

*Freshly squeezed juice
    of 2 lemons*
*1 1/4 to 1 1/2 pounds
    veal scallops*
*1 1/2 cups fine bread
    crumbs*
*1 egg or 2 egg whites,
    slightly beaten*

*4 tablespoons butter or
    margarine, melted, for
    brushing grill*
*1/4 teaspoon each: salt
    and white pepper*

*1/2 pound large mush-
    rooms, cut in half or
    thirds*
*3 large shallots, thinly
    sliced*

1/4 cup minced parsley
*1 tablespoon lemon zest,
    for garnish*
*1 lemon, sliced, for
    garnish*

Sprinkle lemon juice over veal scallops and let stand for 1 hour.

Place bread crumbs on a flat plate. Roll veal in crumbs, then dip in egg and roll in crumbs again.

Preheat stovetop grill. Brush grill surface with butter. Cook veal over medium-high heat about 2 minutes per side or until cooked to taste. Veal will brown slightly on the outside and be just cooked on the inside. Remove to serving dish. Sprinkle with salt and pepper.

Brush grill surface with butter. Grill mushrooms and shallots for 1 to 2 minutes. Turn vegetables as needed to warm and lightly brown. Spoon vegetables next to veal cutlets.

Garnish veal with parsley, lemon zest, and lemon slices. Serve hot. Good with buckwheat noodles.

Makes 4 servings

Cinnamon Veal Chops

■ Marinade

1/2 cup extra virgin
   olive oil
Freshly squeezed juice
   of 1 lime
3 tablespoons chopped
   mint
1/2 teaspoon ground
   cinnamon

4 veal chops, cut
   1/2 inch thick

1 lime, sliced, for
   garnish

Cinnamon used as a flavoring with meats may be new to you, but it adds a pleasant and distinctive taste.

Combine marinade ingredients in a bowl. Pour marinade into a large resealable plastic bag.

Add chops to marinade. Seal the bag securely and turn 2 or 3 times to coat the veal. Refrigerate and marinate veal chops 2 to 3 hours, turning bag occasionally. Drain chops and reserve marinade.

Preheat grill over medium heat. Grill chops about 2 minutes per side or until done to taste and golden brown on the outside. Turn chops once during grilling. Brush chops with reserved marinade as you turn them. Remove veal chops to serving platter. Garnish with lime slices. Good with spinach and grilled corn.

Makes 4 servings

Grilled Veal Chops
with Red Currants

■ Orange Marinade

3/4 cup freshly
   squeezed orange juice
1/4 cup extra virgin
   olive oil
1/2 teaspoon ground
   cinnamon
3 tablespoons minced
   parsley

6 veal loin chops, cut
   about 1/2 inch thick

■ Red Currant Sauce

3 tablespoons butter or
   margarine
1 small onion, minced
Reserved orange mari-
   nade
1 1/4 cups chicken stock
3/4 cup red currant jelly
1/4 teaspoon each: salt,
   white pepper, and
   cinnamon

1/2 cup fresh currants,
   (optional) if avail-
   able, for garnish

Veal is often difficult to obtain outside of larger cities. You may need to order veal ahead from your butcher or meat department if you plan to entertain. When purchasing veal, look for soft, finely-grained, moist flesh that can vary in color from off-white to palest pink. The best quality chops are loin chops.

Fresh red currants are available in limited quantities from June through August. Currants are sweet-tart berries, excellent for jams and jellies. My husband raises red currants in his garden, and when we outsmart the chipmunks, we usually gather enough currants to make this jelly sauce and some jam.

Combine juice, oil, cinnamon, and parsley. Pour into large resealable plastic bag. Add veal chops and turn bag to coat chops. Refrigerate and marinate veal chops 2 to 3 hours, turning bag occasionally. Drain and reserve marinade.

To make sauce, heat butter in saucepan over medium heat. Sauté onion for 4 minutes, stirring often. Add reserved marinade and continue cooking until liquid is reduced to about 3 to 4 tablespoons. Mix in chicken stock and jelly. Cook for 4 minutes, stirring often. Season with salt, pepper, and cinnamon. Set aside.

Preheat stovetop grill. Cook veal chops over medium-high heat, 2 minutes each side, or until chops have browned slightly on the outside and are done to taste on the inside. Do not overcook veal. Cover chops with currant sauce and serve with fresh currants as a garnish.

Makes 6 servings

Grilled Ham with Curried Apricots

Curried Apricots

1 large can (16 oz)
   apricots, drained, pits
   discarded
1/2 cup golden raisins
3 tablespoons butter or
   margarine, cut in 1/2-
   inch pieces
1/4 cup firmly packed
   brown sugar
1 tablespoon curry
   powder
1/8 teaspoon ground
   cinnamon
1/2 cup macaroons or
   other cookie crumbs

1/4 cup firmly packed
   dark brown sugar
1 teaspoon Dijon mus-
   tard
1 tablespoon red wine
   vinegar
1 slice boiled ham, 1/2
   inch thick, cut in half

Curry is customarily thought of as hot and spicy. However, dozens of quite distinct types of curry are available in specialty food shops. Curry powder is a blending of many kinds of spices and herbs, but it is turmeric that gives curry powder a distinctive color and chili powders that control its hotness. For this recipe, use a commercial curry powder. I have used canned fruit combined with curry powder and brown sugar, then baked. This combination makes a simple but elegant sauce.

Preheat oven to 375° F. To make curried apricots, mix apricots and raisins in a casserole dish. Sprinkle with butter. Mix sugar, curry powder, and cinnamon in a small bowl. Sprinkle with macaroon crumbs.

Bake uncovered for 20 minutes, stirring twice. Serve warm.

When ready to grill the ham slices, mix together sugar, mustard, and vinegar. Sprinkle and press sugar mixture onto ham slices.

Preheat grill. Grill ham slices over medium-high heat about 1 to 2 minutes on each side or until ham is warm and sugar melts. Put a slice of ham on each plate and serve with warm curried apricots.

Makes 2 servings

Ham Steak with Red-Eye Gravy

■ Red-Eye Gravy

4 tablespoons butter or margarine
1/2 cup firmly packed dark brown sugar
1/2 cup strong black coffee

1 slice boiled ham, 1/2 inch thick
Butter or margarine, for brushing grill

Melt butter in saucepan. Whisk sugar into pan, cook over low heat, stirring constantly until sugar melts. Stir in coffee, simmer 4 minutes. Gravy will be red-brown in color. Set gravy aside.

Cut ham into 2-inch slices.

Preheat stovetop grill. Brush grill surface with butter. Grill ham over medium-high heat about 1 minute on each side. Ham will brown slightly and be warm. Remove ham to individual plates. Drizzle with hot red-eye gravy. Good with grilled apples and baked beans.

Makes 2 to 3 servings

Garlic Steak

2 cloves garlic, minced
1/2 teaspoon freshly ground black pepper
Peanut oil, for brushing steaks

1 large clove garlic (use elephant garlic if available), sliced horizontally
2 well-trimmed shell steaks or T-bone steaks, cut 1/2 to 3/4 inch thick

Mix garlic and pepper with oil. Brush steaks with flavored oil.

Cut elephant garlic into thin horizontal slices. Set aside.

Preheat grill. Cook steaks over high heat, 2 minutes per side. Set elephant garlic slices on top of the steaks. Cover grill with lid. Reduce heat to medium-high and continue cooking for about 3 to 4 minutes, or until steak is done to taste. To test for doneness, remove a steak to a plate. Cut into the steak and see if it is done for your individual taste. If not, return steak to grill and continue cooking until done. It may be necessary to turn steak again during grilling. Remove steak to a plate. Serve steaks whole or slice and serve hot.

Makes 2 servings

Pepper Steak

1 flank steak, about 1 to 1 1/2 pounds
2 large red or green bell peppers
1 large onion

1/4 teaspoon each: garlic powder and dried basil
Peanut oil, for brushing meat and vegetables
Salt and pepper, to taste

Cut steak into 1/2- to 3/4-inch strips across the grain. Cut the peppers in half, discard the seeds, and slice the peppers into 1/2-inch strips. Slice the onion into 1/2-inch rounds.

Mix the garlic powder and basil into the peanut oil.

Preheat stovetop grill. Cook flank steak strips over medium-high heat. Brush meat with flavored oil and turn meat once or twice until cooked to taste, about 2 to 3 minutes per side. Do not overcook. Meat will brown on the outside and is best served rare to medium. Remove steak strips to serving bowl.

Quickly grill pepper strips and onion rings over high heat, brushing vegetables with flavored oil as you grill. Turn vegetables frequently until they have softened and peppers char slightly.

Toss vegetables with flank steak strips. Season to taste with salt and pepper. Serve hot. Good with brown rice.

Makes 4 servings

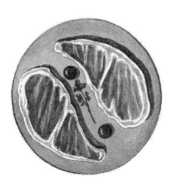

SAUSAGES AND BURGERS

■ I have included this short chapter as a truly enjoyable way to use the stovetop grill.

■ These sausage and burger recipes are inexpensive, simple, and perfect for children and casual entertaining.

■ The recipe for Basil Potato Salad (p. 91) included here works well as a side dish with all of these sausage and burger meals.

Miniature Hot Dogs with Mustard and Currant Jelly

1/4 cup Dijon mustard
1 cup currant jelly
3 tablespoons water

1 pound miniature
   hot dogs
Toothpicks

This recipe makes an easy but marvelous lunch.

Combine mustard, jelly, and water in small saucepan. Cook over medium-high heat until mixture is blended, about 3 minutes, stirring often. Cool. Pour sauce into a deep bowl.

Mix in hot dogs, turning so all surfaces are coated in mustard sauce.

Preheat stovetop grill. Cook hot dogs at medium-high for 3 to 4 minutes, turning once or twice. Hot dogs will be cooked thoroughly and slightly charred on the outside.

Place hot dogs on plate and serve with toothpicks. Serve with gherkin pickles and Basil Potato Salad (recipe follows).

Makes 4 servings

Basil Potato Salad

6 to 7 large potatoes (about 2 lb) washed

4 strips lean bacon, cut into thirds
1 medium red onion, minced

1/4 cup cider vinegar
2 tablespoons minced basil
1/4 teaspoon white pepper
3/4 cup mayonnaise

Slide potatoes into boiling, salted water and cook over medium heat until potatoes are just fork tender. Run cold water over potatoes, peel, and cube. Put potatoes in a deep bowl.

Preheat grill. Cook bacon over medium-high heat, turning as needed. Bacon should be crisp. Remove bacon and crumble. Toss bacon bits and onion with potatoes.

In a separate bowl, mix vinegar, basil, pepper, and mayonnaise. Toss potatoes with dressing. Cover and let stand for 1 hour before serving. Toss potato salad again and serve.

Makes 6 to 8 servings

Smoked Sausage and Apple Slices on Sauerkraut

2 large Golden or Red Delicious apples
3 cups sauerkraut, drained
1/2 teaspoon caraway seeds
1/4 cup grated carrots
1/2 teaspoon each: salt and dried thyme
1/4 teaspoon pepper
1/2 cup dry white wine

1 pound smoked sausage, cut in 3-inch diagonal pieces, 1/2 inch thick

This recipe from the Alsace province of France works wonderfully well for football parties.

Peel and core apples and cut into thin slices.

Heat sauerkraut in a saucepan over medium heat. Mix in caraway seeds, carrots, and apples, stirring often. Add salt, thyme, pepper, and wine; blend all ingredients together. Simmer about 3 minutes. Remove from heat and spread in a casserole dish.

Preheat stovetop grill. Cook over medium-high heat about 1 to 1 1/2 minutes on each side. Sausage should be hot and golden brown. Remove sausage and mix with hot sauerkraut. Serve at once. Good with salad and French bread.

Makes 4 to 6 servings

Grilled Italian Sausage

■ *Tomato Brushing Sauce*

1 can (8 oz) tomato sauce
2 tablespoons water
1/2 teaspoon each: dried marjoram, dried rosemary, garlic powder, and dried oregano

4 mild Italian sausages, cut in half horizontally

To make brushing sauce, combine tomato sauce, water, marjoram, rosemary, garlic powder, and oregano. Simmer in a saucepan for 4 minutes, stirring often. Remove sauce from heat and reserve.

Cut sausages in half horizontally. Preheat grill. Cook sausages over medium-high heat, cut side down, for 2 minutes. Brush liberally with sauce. Turn sausages over, brush again with sauce, and continue grilling for 2 minutes or until sausages are cooked through. Remove to serving dish. Serve sausages hot with extra sauce and garlic bread. Good also as a first course.

Makes 4 servings

Bratwurst with Beer Mustard

■ *Beer Mustard*

*6 tablespoons dry
    mustard*
1/3 cup beer
*1/4 teaspoon white
    horseradish, optional*

4 bratwurst
*1 can beer, less 1/3 cup
    used above for beer
    mustard*
4 hot dog rolls
4 pickles, sliced

Beer mustard is easy to make. Using various types of beers will yield subtle taste variations in the mustard. Experiment to create a beer mustard that you truly enjoy.

To make mustard, mix dry mustard, 1/3 cup beer, and horseradish together in a small bowl. Let mustard stand for 15 minutes. Stir the mustard before serving. If mustard is too thick, add beer by the tablespoon until desired consistency is obtained.

Cut bratwurst in half horizontally. Pour remaining beer into a bowl. Marinate bratwurst in beer for 1 hour. Drain and discard marinade.

Preheat grill. Cook bratwurst, cut side down, for 2 minutes over medium-high heat. Turn bratwurst over and continue grilling for 2 minutes or until cooked through. Remove from grill.

Warm rolls, cut side down, on the grill. To serve, place 2 halves of the bratwurst on a warm hot dog roll. Serve with pickles, mustard, baked beans and, of course, cold beer.

Makes 4 servings

Breakfast Sausage with Pear Relish

■ Pear Relish

3 firm, ripe pears, cored, chopped

3 tablespoons freshly squeezed lime juice

1 cup drained mandarin oranges

1 small red onion, chopped

3 stalks celery, minced

2 teaspoons minced orange zest

1 tablespoon minced mint

1/8 teaspoon hot-pepper flakes

6 slices prepared breakfast sausages, cut 1/2 inch thick

Pear relish is good to make in the fall and winter when pears are fresh and plentiful.

Place pears in a bowl and toss with lime juice. Add oranges, red onion, celery, orange zest, mint, and hot-pepper flakes. Toss ingredients lightly. Cover and refrigerate until needed. Pear relish can be made the day before serving.

Preheat stovetop grill. Grill sausage slices over medium-high heat until done, about 1 1/2 to 2 minutes on each side. Sausage will be crisp, firm on the outside, and cooked through on the inside. Turn sausage once while grilling. Remove sausage to serving plate. Put pear relish on side of plate and serve with Blueberry Breakfast Bread (recipe follows).

Makes 6 servings

Blueberry Breakfast Bread

1/4 cup butter or
   margarine
3/4 cup sugar
1 egg
2 cups unbleached
   all-purpose flour,
   reserve 1/4 cup
1 teaspoon baking
   powder
1 teaspoon baking soda
1/2 teaspoon each: salt
   and ground cinnamon
1/2 cup buttermilk
3/4 cup fresh
   blueberries, washed,
   patted dry, or thawed
   frozen berries,
   drained

Grease a 9- by 9- by 3-inch pan. Preheat oven to 400° F.

Cream butter and sugar together in large bowl of electric mixer. Beat in egg. Add dry ingredients alternately with buttermilk. Mix only until batter is smooth.

Toss remaining 1/4 cup flour with blueberries in a bowl. Fold berries into batter.

Pour batter into prepared pan. Bake for 20 to 25 minutes.

Let bread stand 5 minutes. Remove from pan. Cool blueberry bread on wire rack. Serve at room temperature.

Hamburgers with Olive Salsa

■ Olive Salsa

2 medium tomatoes,
  seeded, chopped
2 cloves garlic, minced
1 small onion, minced
1/4 teaspoon chopped
  cilantro
1/8 teaspoon each: salt
  and pepper
1/3 cup chopped green
  olives

1 pound ground beef
1/2 teaspoon powdered
  garlic
1/4 cup chopped green
  olives
Salt and pepper to taste

4 sesame seed ham-
  burger rolls
4 lettuce leaves

The olives in this recipe give both the burgers and the salsa a new dimension I think you'll love.

Combine salsa ingredients in a bowl. Cover and refrigerate until serving time. Toss before serving.

Mix ground beef, garlic, olives, salt, and pepper. Shape into 4 hamburger patties about 1/2 inch thick.

Preheat stovetop grill. Cook hamburgers, over medium-high heat until done to taste, about 2 to 3 minutes per side. Turn burgers once or twice during grilling.

Warm rolls, cut side down, on the grill. Place each roll on a plate. Set a lettuce leaf on the bottom and the burger on top. Serve hamburgers hot with olive salsa on the side.

Makes 4 servings

Lamb Burgers with Feta Cheese

**1 pound lean ground
lamb**
**1/2 pound lean ground
beef**
1 egg
**1/2 pita pocket, ground
into crumbs**
**1 1/2 tablespoons dried
oregano**
2 cloves garlic, minced
1 small onion, minced
**1/2 teaspoon freshly
ground black pepper**
1/4 cup chopped parsley

**6 ounces feta cheese,
crumbled**
**1/2 cup sliced black
olives**

These tasty burgers come to life with the addition of the flavorful feta, or goat, cheese.
For best results, grind your own meat or ask your butcher to custom grind it for you.

Mix lamb and beef with egg, crumbs, oregano, garlic, onion, pepper, and parsley. Shape into 6 burgers. Chill until ready to grill.

Preheat stovetop grill. Grill burgers over high heat until golden brown on the outside and medium done on the inside, or to taste. Turn burgers as necessary.

Remove lamb burgers to serving dish. Sprinkle with crumbled feta cheese and olives. Serve burgers hot with warm whole wheat pita bread.

Makes 5 to 6 servings

German Meatballs

3/4 pound each: ground
    pork and ground veal
1 egg, slightly beaten
3/4 cup fine bread
    crumbs
1 medium onion, minced
1 teaspoon lemon zest
1/2 teaspoon each: salt
    and dried tarragon
1/4 teaspoon fresh
    ground pepper

Sauce

2 cups beef stock
1 tablespoon freshly
    squeezed lemon juice
2 tablespoons corn-
    starch
1/4 cup capers, drained

Mix pork and veal together in a deep mixing bowl. Blend in egg, bread crumbs, onion, lemon zest, salt, tarragon, and pepper. Shape into 2-inch patties. Place on dish and refrigerate until ready to grill.

To prepare sauce, heat stock over medium heat until just simmering . Remove 2 tablespoons stock and combine with lemon juice and cornstarch. Return mixture to stock and continue simmering until sauce thickens. Stir in capers.

Preheat stovetop grill. Cook meat patties about 4 to 5 minutes over medium-high heat, turning once. Meat will be crusty on the outside and cooked to taste on the inside.

Ladle sauce over patties on serving dish. Good served hot with red cabbage, grilled apples, and pumpernickel bread.

Makes 4 to 6 servings

Cheeseburgers

1 pound ground beef
1 egg
1/2 cup bread crumbs
1 tablespoon mustard
1/4 teaspoon pepper

4 slices American cheese
4 hamburger rolls, split

Combine beef, egg, bread crumbs, mustard, and pepper. Shape into 4 patties.

Preheat stovetop grill. Cook burgers over medium-high heat. Turn once or twice until rare. Add a slice of cheese on top of each burger. Cook 1 minute longer. Serve hot burgers on rolls that have been warmed, cut side down, on the grill.

Makes 4 servings

CHICKEN AND TURKEY

■ Versatility and reasonable cost have long made chicken one of the most popular entrées. Recently, the interest in foods lower in fat has emphasized another positive aspect to the grilling and enjoyment of both chicken and turkey.

■ The fast-cooking nature of the stovetop grill lends itself to the use of chicken breasts, kabobs, strips, and wing recipes. Prepared on the grill, they are tender and delicious, and they cook evenly and thoroughly.

■ One new concept for adding flavor that I have used in this chapter is placing citrus or herbs under the skin of chicken breasts. Select chicken breasts with the skin still on. Separate the skin from the breast with your fingers and slide fruit slices or herbs under the skin before grilling with the skin on. This technique gives a terrific flavor to grilled chicken.

Grilled Chicken Breast Sandwich

■ **Brushing Sauce**

1/2 cup chili sauce
2 tablespoons molasses
1/2 teaspoon dry
* mustard*
2 tablespoons freshly
* squeezed orange juice*

2 whole chicken breasts,
* skinned, boned*

4 burger buns or rolls,
* split*
4 lettuce leaves
4 tomato slices

1 onion, thinly sliced
Sliced pickles

This sandwich has gained immense popularity recently. Versions of it have been added to many menus, from fast food restaurants to gourmet sandwich shops. Now you can make it simply, quickly, and deliciously at home using the stovetop grill.

Combine sauce ingredients in a bowl.

Flatten chicken pieces between 2 sheets of waxed paper, using a spatula or mallet. Arrange chicken in a flat glass bowl and brush with sauce.

Preheat stovetop grill. Cook chicken over medium-high heat until done, about 3 to 5 minutes, turning once. Chicken will be slightly firm to the touch. Remove chicken from grill.

Arrange lettuce leaf on bottom side of bun. Put chicken breast on lettuce. Top chicken with tomato and onion slices. Serve hot with pickles.

Makes 4 servings

New York State Chicken Wings with Blue Cheese Dipping Sauce

■ Blue Cheese Dipping Sauce

1 cup mayonnaise
3 cloves garlic, minced
1 small onion, minced
1/4 cup minced fresh parsley
1/2 cup sour cream or low-fat, plain yogurt
1 tablespoon freshly squeezed lemon juice
1 tablespoon white vinegar
1/3 cup crumbled blue cheese, or to taste
Salt and freshly ground black pepper to taste

■ Chicken Wings

2 dozen chicken wings, tips removed, cut at joint
Salt and pepper
Peanut oil, for brushing grill

2 tablespoons peanut oil
2 tablespoons hot sauce
1 tablespoon white vinegar

1 bunch of celery, trimmed, cut into celery sticks

Wing tips can be saved, frozen, and used in future chicken stock preparation.

Mix sauce ingredients in a bowl. Cover and refrigerate until serving time. Stir before serving.

Sprinkle chicken wing pieces with salt and pepper.

Preheat stovetop grill to medium-high heat. Brush grill surface lightly with peanut oil. Cook chicken wings 5 to 6 minutes, turning as necessary. Cover grill with lid after 2 minutes of grilling. Chicken is done when slightly firm to the touch and when juices run clear if chicken is cut with a knife. Remove wings from grill and arrange on serving dish.

Heat oil in small saucepan. Blend in hot sauce and vinegar. Remove pan from heat. Pour over chicken wings. Serve chicken wings hot with celery sticks and Blue Cheese Dipping Sauce.

Makes 4 servings

Chicken with Orange Slices under the Skin

4 orange slices

■ **Orange Marinade**

1/3 cup extra virgin olive oil
1/4 cup freshly squeezed orange juice
1 clove garlic, minced
1/2 teaspoon dried rosemary
1/4 teaspoon cayenne
2 tablespoons minced parsley

2 whole chicken breasts, skin intact, boned

1/4 cup minced parsley for garnish

Cut 4 very thin slices from center of orange and set aside. Use the remainder of the orange for juice for marinade.

Combine marinade ingredients in a bowl. Pour marinade into resealable plastic bag. Cut chicken breasts in half, place in bag, seal bag securely, and turn several times, so chicken is thoroughly coated by marinade. Refrigerate and marinate chicken for 1 hour. Drain and discard marinade.

Loosen skin on chicken breast. Slide 1 thin slice of orange between skin and chicken. Pat skin back into position.

Preheat stovetop grill. Cook chicken, skin side down, over medium-high heat for 4 to 6 minutes, turning once. Chicken is done when slightly firm to the touch and juices run clear when chicken is cut with a knife. Remove chicken from grill and place on individual dishes. Sprinkle with parsley. Serve hot with Wild Rice salad (recipe follows).

Makes 4 servings

Wild Rice Salad

4 cups chicken stock
1 cup wild rice
1 1/2 cups long-grain white rice
2 cups chopped red bell pepper

1/2 cup safflower oil
1/4 cup red wine vinegar
1 tablespoon Worcestershire sauce
1/4 teaspoon freshly ground pepper

3 cups water
1 cup fresh peas

1 large red Spanish onion, sliced, separated into rings

Wild rice salad works well as a side dish with chicken and turkey. It can be prepared ahead of time, and it works well served warm or cold.

Place stock in large saucepan and bring to a boil over high heat. Stir in wild rice and bring to a boil again. Cover, reduce heat to low, and simmer 40 minutes. Stir white rice into mixture and continue to simmer 15 to 20 minutes or until all liquid is absorbed. Remove from heat and let cool.

Place cooled rice mixture in large serving bowl. Mix in red pepper.

In a small bowl, whisk oil, vinegar, Worcestershire sauce, and pepper together. When completely blended, pour over rice mixture and toss.

Bring the water to a boil in a small saucepan. Add peas and cook for 1 minute or until peas turn bright green. Drain into a strainer and immediately rinse under cold running water. Arrange peas in a wreath atop rice mixture. Place onion rings in center of pea wreath. Serve warm or cold.

Makes 6 to 8 servings

Chicken with Brandy Sauce

■ **Brandy Sauce**

1/4 cup brandy
1 egg
1 teaspoon orange zest
2 tablespoons freshly
  squeezed orange juice
1/2 cup butter or marga-
  rine, melted
1/4 teaspoon salt
1/8 teaspoon white
  pepper
1/2 cup whipped cream

2 chicken breasts, skin
  intact, boned
2 tablespoons butter
  or margarine, for
  brushing chicken

To make the sauce, blend all ingredients in a food processor fitted with a steel blade. Set aside on a warmer or in very low oven.

Cut each chicken breast in half. Brush chicken with butter.

Preheat grill. Cook chicken over medium-high heat for 5 to 6 minutes, skin side down. Turn once during grilling. Chicken is cooked when it is slightly firm to the touch and when the juices run clear when chicken is cut with a knife.

To serve, place chicken piece, skin side up, on each plate, and drizzle with sauce. Serve hot. Good with French bread and Wild Rice Salad (see page 105).

Makes 4 servings

Spanish-Style Chicken

■ Raisin Wine Sauce

2 tablespoons extra
   virgin olive oil
2 tablespoons butter or
   margarine
1 large onion, chopped
1/2 pound mushrooms,
   sliced
2 tablespoons
   unbleached all-
   purpose flour
3/4 cup dry white wine
3/4 cup chicken stock
1 1/2 tablespoons
   freshly squeezed
   lemon juice
2 bay leaves
1/4 teaspoon each dried
   thyme, salt, and
   pepper
1/2 cup raisins

2 whole chicken breasts,
   skinned, boned

1/2 teaspoon dried
   thyme
Extra virgin oil, for
   brushing chicken

Determining the age of the bay leaves, which are commonly sold bottled or boxed in the spice sections of super-markets, is difficult. Old bay leaves will have lost their flavor, making them ineffective. Bay leaves should always be discarded before a dish is served.

To prepare wine sauce, heat oil and butter in saucepan. Sauté onion and mushrooms for 4 minutes over medium heat, stirring occasionally. Stir in flour and continue cooking 2 minutes. Stir in white wine and chicken stock. Bring mixture to a boil. Simmer sauce, stirring constantly, until sauce thickens. Mix in lemon juice, bay leaves, thyme, salt, pepper, and raisins. Simmer 5 minutes. Taste to adjust seasonings. Remove from heat and discard bay leaves.

Cut chicken breasts in 1/2-inch strips.

Preheat stovetop grill. Stir thyme into oil. Brush chicken strips with flavored oil. Grill chicken over medium-high heat about 3 minutes on each side, or until done to taste. Chicken is done when it is slightly firm to the touch and juices run clear if chicken is cut with a knife.

Remove chicken to individual plates. Drizzle sauce over chicken. Serve hot. Good with gazpacho as a first course and flan for dessert.

Makes 4 servings

Chicken Breasts with Mushrooms

■ *Sage Marinade*

*1/2 cup extra virgin
    olive oil*
*1/4 cup freshly
    squeezed lemon juice*
1/2 teaspoon dried sage
2 bay leaves

*2 whole chicken breasts,
    skin intact, boned*
*3/4 cup sliced mush-
    rooms*
1/2 teaspoon dried sage

Sage marinade has a powerfully aromatic quality.

Combine marinade ingredients in a bowl. Pour marinade into resealable plastic bag. Cut chicken breasts in half, place in bag, and seal the bag securely. Turn bag a few times so all portions of chicken are coated by marinade. Refrigerate and marinate for 1 hour. Drain, discard marinade.

Separate skin from chicken. Toss mushrooms with sage. Slide mushrooms under the skin. Replace skin.

Preheat stovetop grill. Cook chicken over medium-high heat, skin side down, for about 5 minutes, turning once. Chicken will be slightly firm to the touch and juices will run clear when chicken is cut with a knife.

Remove chicken to serving dish. Serve chicken hot with Mushroom Cornbread (recipe follows).

Makes 4 servings

Mushroom Cornbread

3 lean bacon slices, cut in half

6 tablespoons butter or margarine, melted
1 cup sliced mushrooms

3/4 cup yellow cornmeal
1/4 cup unbleached all-purpose flour
2 tablespoons baking powder
1/2 teaspoon each: baking soda and salt
1 egg
1/2 cup buttermilk

An all-time favorite, this cornbread side dish is very easy to make.

Grease an 8- by 8-inch baking pan. Set aside. Preheat oven to 400° F.

Preheat stovetop grill. Cook bacon strips on medium-high grill until crisp, turning bacon as needed.

Crumble bacon and place in a non-stick frying pan. Heat 2 tablespoons butter. Add mushrooms and sauté over medium heat until tender, about 5 minutes, stirring often.

Mix cornmeal, flour, baking powder, baking soda, and salt in a bowl. Blend in egg, buttermilk, and remaining butter. Do not overbeat. Mixture should be just combined. Mix in mushrooms and bacon.

Spoon batter into prepared pan. Bake 18 to 20 minutes or until inserted bread tester comes out dry. Cool cornbread on wire rack. Cut into 6 pieces.

Makes 6 servings

Chicken Spears with Avocado Salsa

■ Avocado Salsa

1 large ripe avocado, peeled, and diced
Freshly squeezed juice of 2 limes
2 medium tomatoes, seeded and chopped
4 green onions, minced
1 green bell pepper seeded, chopped
1/4 cup minced cilantro
2 tablespoons extra virgin olive oil
1/2 teaspoon ground cumin
1/4 teaspoon each: salt and hot-pepper flakes

■ Chicken Spears

2 whole chicken breasts, skinned, boned
16 bamboo skewers, soaked in water 10 minutes, drained
1/2 cup freshly squeezed lime juice
1/4 cup extra virgin olive oil
1/2 teaspoon ground cumin
1/4 teaspoon hot-pepper flakes

Make this salsa to your own taste; you can make it spicier or milder to suit your own family or company. Salsa is a marvelous sauce for a wide variety of chicken dishes.

Toss avocado with lime juice in a bowl. Mix in tomatoes, onions, pepper, and cilantro. Toss with olive oil, cumin, salt, and hot-pepper flakes. Cover lightly and refrigerate until serving time. Toss salsa again before serving. Adjust seasonings to taste.

Cut chicken breasts into 8 strips each. Thread chicken onto skewers. Place in a flat dish. Mix lime juice, olive oil, cumin, and hot-pepper flakes. Brush chicken with marinade. Let chicken marinate for 1 hour. Drain and discard marinade.

Preheat stovetop grill. Cook chicken skewers over medium-high heat for about 6 minutes or until chicken is cooked, turning as needed.

Chicken is done when slightly firm to the touch and when juices run clear if the chicken is cut with a knife. Serve with tortillas and refried beans (recipe follows).

Makes 4 servings

Refried Beans

1 pound dried pinto or red kidney beans

5 strips lean bacon, cut in half
1/2 teaspoon each: ground cumin, salt, and garlic powder
1/4 teaspoon each: pepper and hot-pepper flakes

Grilling the bacon for the side dish of refried beans cooks the bacon perfectly, while removing most of the excess grease.

Wash beans and place in a large pot. Cover beans with water and bring to a boil. Reduce heat to a simmer and continue cooking for 2 1/2 to 3 hours, uncovered. Add more water, if necessary, and stir beans occasionally. Beans can be prepared the day before serving. When draining beans, set aside 1 1/2 cups of the cooking liquid.

Preheat stovetop grill. Cook bacon over medium-high heat, turning until done to taste. Drain bacon on paper towels. Crumble bacon. Purée beans, using a food processor fitted with a steel blade, or use a potato masher.

Heat reserved cooking liquid and bacon in a large pan. Mix in beans and seasonings. Cook over medium heat until beans are hot. Remove beans from heat.

When ready to serve, heat refried beans in a frying pan, stirring often.

Makes 4 to 6 servings

Chicken with Green Olives

■ Green Olive Sauce

1 tablespoon extra
   virgin olive oil
1 tablespoon butter or
   margarine
2 cloves garlic, minced
1 small onion, minced
1 green bell pepper,
   seeded, chopped
1 can (8 oz) tomato
   sauce
1/2 teaspoon
   Worcestershire sauce
1/4 teaspoon each: hot-
   pepper flakes, salt,
   and sugar
1/2 cup sliced green
   olives

2 whole chicken breasts,
   skinned and boned

Green olives are unripe when picked, and then pickled in brine. They impart a tart taste to the chicken and add color and character to this dish.

To prepare sauce, heat oil and butter in saucepan. Sauté garlic, onion, and pepper for 5 minutes, stirring often. Stir in tomato sauce, Worcestershire sauce, hot-pepper flakes, salt, sugar, and olives. Simmer 5 minutes. Remove from heat.

Cut each chicken breast in half.

Flatten each piece of chicken between 2 sheets of waxed paper with a mallet or spatula. Brush chicken liberally with sauce. Preheat stovetop grill. Cook chicken over medium-high heat, turning once, until chicken is cooked, about 4 to 5 minutes. Brush chicken with sauce as you turn it. Chicken is done when firm to the touch and when juices run clear when the chicken is cut with a knife. Remove to individual dishes. Serve with hot green olive sauce. Good with saffron rice and cornbread.

Makes 4 servings

Chicken with Herbs

■ Herb Stuffing

2 cups fine bread crumbs
2 tablespoons minced parsley
1/2 teaspoon each: dried basil, dried tarragon, and dried thyme
1/4 teaspoon each: salt and pepper

2 whole chicken breasts, skin intact, boned
Extra virgin olive oil, for brushing chicken

Herb stuffing gives a wonderful flavor to chicken breasts and keeps them particularly moist and juicy.

To prepare stuffing, toss bread crumbs with parsley, basil, tarragon, thyme, salt, and pepper.

Loosen skin over chicken. Lightly spoon about 1/4 cup stuffing under skin. Replace skin over chicken. Brush each chicken breast with oil.

Preheat stovetop grill. Grill chicken breasts over medium-high heat, skin side down, for 4 minutes. Turn chicken breasts over and continue grilling for 3 minutes or until chicken is done. Chicken is done when slightly firm to the touch and juices run clear when chicken is cut with a knife. Serve hot with ratatouille or grilled zucchini as a side dish.

Makes 4 servings

Chicken Breasts with Lime Slices under the Skin

■ Lime, Coriander, Yogurt Sauce

1 teaspoon lime zest
2 tablespoons freshly squeezed lime juice
1/2 cup minced coriander
2 cups low-fat, plain yogurt
1 small lime

Butter or margarine, melted, for brushing chicken
2 whole chicken breasts, skin intact, boned

The limes for this recipe should be sliced thinly. After grilling, discard the chicken skins and use fresh slices of lime as a garnish.

To prepare yogurt sauce, blend lime zest, juice, and coriander into yogurt. Spoon sauce into a serving bowl. Cover and refrigerate until serving time. Stir sauce before serving.

Cut 4 paper-thin slices from center of lime. Use remainder of lime for juice for sauce.

Preheat stovetop grill. Cut each chicken breast in half. Loosen skin over chicken. Slide 1 thin slice of lime under the skin of each half of chicken breast. Replace skin over chicken. Brush butter over chicken. Grill over medium-high heat, skin side down, for 3 to 4 minutes. Turn chicken over and continue grilling for 2 to 3 minutes or until chicken is done. Chicken is done when slightly firm to the touch and juices run clear when chicken is cut with a knife.

Serve chicken hot, drizzled with yogurt sauce.

Makes 4 servings

Chicken Fajitas

■ Brushing Sauce

4 green onions, minced
1 teaspoon garlic powder
6 tablespoons dark brown sugar
5 tablespoons red wine vinegar
1 1/2 cups light beer
3 teaspoons prepared mustard

2 whole chicken breasts, skinned, boned
1 large onion, sliced
4 flour tortillas
1/2 cup chopped cilantro

Extra virgin olive oil, for brushing

These fajitas are made with spiced, grilled chicken strips wrapped in warm tortillas. They are especially popular with children or guests of all ages.

To prepare brushing sauce, combine all ingredients in a saucepan. Simmer 4 to 5 minutes, stirring occasionally. Remove from heat.

Cut chicken breasts into 1-inch strips.

Place chicken strips in a shallow glass dish. Brush chicken liberally with sauce. Marinate for 1 hour.

Preheat stovetop grill. Cook chicken strips over medium-high heat for 5 to 6 minutes, turning as needed, or until chicken is slightly firm to the touch and juices run clear when chicken is cut with a knife. Remove strips to a bowl.

Brush onion slices with oil, and grill for about 45 seconds to 1 minute on each side.

To serve, warm tortillas on each side over hot grill. Lay tortilla flat, place chicken strips in center, and sprinkle with onions and cilantro. Roll tortillas and serve hot. Good with refried beans.

Makes 4 servings

Cashew Chicken with Yogurt Marinade

■ Yogurt Marinade

1 cup low-fat, plain yogurt
2 teaspoons minced fresh ginger
1/4 teaspoon each: white pepper, ground cardamom, and ground allspice

■ Cashew Sauce

2 tablespoons butter or margarine
1 small onion, minced
2 cloves garlic, minced
1/2 cup roasted cashews
1/4 teaspoon each: ground cardamom, chili powder, and turmeric
1 1/2 cups low-fat, plain yogurt

2 chicken breasts, skin intact, boned
1/2 cup chopped cashews for garnish

Yogurt has gained tremendous popularity in recent years. This yogurt marinade keeps the chicken moist and adds a subtle but distinctive flavor.

Cardamom, a member of the ginger family, is native to East India. The dried seed pods of the cardamom plant are sold in stores as the spice cardamom.

Combine marinade ingredients in a bowl. Spoon into a resealable plastic bag. Cut chicken breasts in half, place in bag, and seal bag securely. Turn bag several times so chicken is completely coated by marinade. Refrigerate and marinate for 1 1/2 hours. Drain and discard marinade.

While chicken is marinating, prepare the cashew sauce. Heat the butter in a saucepan; sauté onion, garlic, nuts, and spices for 5 minutes, stirring occasionally. Cool. Purée mixture in a food processor fitted with a steel blade. Blend mixture into yogurt. Stir to combine ingredients. Set aside until needed.

Preheat stovetop grill. Cook each chicken piece over medium-high heat, skin side down first, for about 5 minutes, turning chicken pieces once during grilling. Chicken is done when slightly firm to the touch and juices run clear when chicken is cut with a knife.

Remove chicken pieces to individual plates. Drizzle chicken with warm cashew sauce. Sprinkle with chopped cashews and serve hot with rice.

Makes 4 servings

Chicken Kabobs with Peach Glaze

■ *Peach Glaze*

2 cups peach juice
1/2 teaspoon curry powder
1/4 teaspoon each: ground cinnamon, chili powder, and ground allspice
2 tablespoons cornstarch

4 bamboo skewers, soaked in water 10 minutes, drained
4 peaches, cut into quarters
4 green onions, cut into 2-inch lengths
2 green bell peppers, seeded, cut into 2-inch pieces
1 pound boneless, skinless chicken breasts, cut into 1-inch pieces

Peanut oil, for brushing grill

I have used fresh peaches to make this glaze. Always choose firm, bright-colored peaches. Green or very hard peaches are immature and will not ripen well.

To make peach glaze, heat peach juice to a boil in saucepan. Mix in curry powder, ground cinnamon, chili powder, and allspice. Remove 3 tablespoons of the juice; mix with cornstarch. Return cornstarch mixture to saucepan. Reduce heat and simmer about 4 to 5 minutes or until sauce thickens. Remove from heat and set aside.

Thread skewers alternately with pieces of peach, green onion, pepper, and chicken. Brush each kabob generously with peach glaze.

Preheat stovetop grill. Brush grill surface lightly with peanut oil. Grill kabobs over medium-high heat, rotating every 2 minutes, until done. Chicken is done when slightly firm to the touch and juices run clear when chicken is cut with a knife. Remove kabobs to serving dish. Serve hot with noodles.

Makes 4 servings

Spicy Chicken with Green Pepper and Peanuts

■ Marinade

2 egg whites, slightly beaten
1 tablespoon cornstarch
1/4 teaspoon each: salt and garlic powder
1/8 teaspoon white pepper

2 chicken breasts, skinned, boned

■ Sauce

3 tablespoons peanut oil
2 cloves garlic, minced
1/2 teaspoon freshly grated ginger root
1/4 teaspoon hot-pepper flakes
4 green onions,
1 can sliced bamboo shoots, drained
1 cup sliced green bell pepper strips
1/2 cup unsalted roasted peanuts
3 tablespoons soy sauce
2 tablespoons dry white wine
1/2 teaspoon sugar
Peanut oil, for brushing grill

The following six chicken recipes are Asian in style, taste, and character.

You can use either of the two major types of peanuts, Spanish or Virginia, for this recipe. The hot-pepper flakes called for here can be used liberally or conservatively, according to your own preference for fiery flavoring.

Combine all marinade ingredients in shallow bowl. Cut chicken breasts in half and then into 4 or 5 strips. Add chicken pieces to marinade. Refrigerate for 1 hour.

While chicken is marinating, prepare sauce. Heat oil. Sauté garlic, ginger, and hot-pepper flakes in saucepan for 1 minute. Add green onions and continue cooking over medium-high heat for 2 minutes, stirring often. Mix in bamboo shoots, pepper strips, and peanuts; cook for 1 minute. Stir in soy sauce, wine, and sugar. Cook until sauce is hot and ingredients are combined. Remove from heat and reserve.

Preheat stovetop grill. Brush grill surface lightly with oil. Cook chicken strips for about 4 or 5 minutes over medium-high heat. Turn chicken strips once or twice during grilling. Chicken is done when it is slightly firm to the touch and juices run clear when chicken is cut with a knife. Remove chicken strips and mound in the center of serving dish. Top with hot sauce. Serve at once. Good with rice or noodles.

Makes 4 servings

Thai Chicken Kabobs with Coconut Sauce

■ Coconut Sauce

1 cup canned,
    unsweetened coconut
    milk
1 teaspoon ground curry
1/2 cup smooth peanut
    butter
1/4 cup sugar
3 tablespoons white
    vinegar
2 tablespoons corn-
    starch

■ Kabobs

2 whole chicken breasts,
    skinned, boned
1 cup freshly squeezed
    lime juice
1 teaspoon lime zest
4 8-inch bamboo
    skewers, soaked in
    water for 10 minutes,
    drained

Peanut oil, for brushing
    chicken and grill

1/4 cup freshly grated
    coconut, for garnish

Coconut is a very important ingredient in Southeast Asian cooking. Coconut meat is available fresh or in jars and cans in specialty shops.

To prepare coconut sauce, blend coconut milk and powdered curry together in a saucepan. Bring to a boil. Reduce heat to simmer and blend in peanut butter, sugar, and vinegar mixed with cornstarch. Simmer until smooth (about 2 minutes), stirring often. Sauce will thicken slightly. Remove from heat. Serve sauce hot.

Cut chicken breasts into 1-inch pieces.

Marinate chicken pieces in freshly squeezed lime juice and lime zest for 1 hour. Drain chicken and thread onto skewers. Brush chicken kabobs with peanut oil.

Preheat grill. Brush grill surface lightly with oil. Grill chicken kabobs over medium-high heat for about 3 to 4 minutes, turning as necessary to cook all sides of kabobs. Chicken is done when slightly firm to the touch and juices run clear when chicken is cut with a knife.

Place a chicken kabob on each plate, drizzle with coconut sauce, and serve with white rice or fried rice. Garnish with freshly grated coconut.

Makes 4 servings

Lemon Chicken

2 chicken breasts, skin discarded, boned

■ **Lemon Marinade**

1/2 cup freshly squeezed lemon juice
3 tablespoons sherry
1/4 teaspoon salt
1/8 teaspoon white pepper
2 tablespoons minced parsley

■ **Asian Sauce**

2 tablespoons peanut oil
2 cloves garlic, minced
3 green onions, minced
1/3 cup catsup
3 tablespoons soy sauce
1 tablespoon sesame oil
1/4 cup red wine vinegar
1/4 cup dark brown sugar, firmly packed

1/2 head iceberg lettuce
1 cup cherry tomatoes
Peanut oil, for brushing grill
1 lemon, thinly sliced
1/2 cup chopped parsley

The lemon marinade in this recipe makes the chicken tender and moist and imparts a sweet-and-sour flavor.

Cut each chicken breast in half, then cut each piece into 4 strips.

Combine marinade ingredients in a bowl. Pour marinade into resealable plastic bag. Add chicken breasts and seal bag securely. Turn bag several times, so chicken is completely coated by the marinade. Refrigerate and marinate for 1 1/2 hours. Drain and discard marinade.

To prepare sauce, heat peanut oil in a small saucepan. Sauté garlic and onions for 3 minutes, stirring often. Add remaining ingredients and stir to combine. Continue cooking over low heat until sauce is hot. Set aside until ready to serve.

Cut lettuce in bite-sized pieces. Spread lettuce over serving plate. Sprinkle lettuce and edge the plate with cherry tomatoes.

Preheat stovetop grill. Brush grill surface lightly with oil. Cook chicken strips over medium-high heat for about 4 to 5 minutes. Turn once or twice during grilling. Chicken is done when slightly firm to the touch and when juices run clear when chicken is cut with a knife. Remove chicken strips to center of prepared dish. Drizzle with heated sauce and sprinkle with parsley. Garnish with lemon slices. Serve hot with rice or noodles.

Makes 4 servings

Asian Chicken with Black Beans

■ Soy Sauce Marinade

1/2 cup soy sauce
1/4 cup white wine
1 teaspoon sugar
1/4 teaspoon each:
   garlic powder and
   ginger powder

■ Black Bean Sauce

1 tablespoon fermented
   black beans, rinsed,
   drained
1 tablespoon peanut oil
2 cloves garlic, minced
3 green onions, chopped
1/2 cup chicken stock
3 tablespoons dry white
   wine
2 teaspoons soy sauce
1 teaspoon sugar
2 teaspoons cornstarch

2 chicken breasts, skin
   intact, boned

Fermented black beans, sometimes called salted black beans, *are purchased dried and should be washed before using. These beans can usually be found packaged in heavy plastic bags in specialty markets. Purchase black beans that feel soft and supple through the package.*

Combine marinade ingredients and pour into resealable plastic bag. Add chicken pieces and seal bag securely. Turn bag several times so chicken is completely coated by the marinade. Refrigerate and marinate for 1 hour. Drain and discard marinade.

Meanwhile, prepare black bean sauce. Mash beans with the back of a spoon. Heat oil in a wok or saucepan. Fry garlic, beans, and green onions.

Add chicken stock, wine, soy sauce, and sugar to the saucepan. Remove 1 tablespoon of sauce and mix with the cornstarch. Return to saucepan. Continue simmering until sauce thickens slightly, stirring occasionally. Remove sauce from heat.

Preheat stovetop grill. Brush chicken breasts with sauce. Cut chicken breasts in half. Cook chicken over medium-high heat for about 5 minutes, skin side down first. Turn once during grilling. Chicken is done when it is slightly firm to the touch and juices run clear when chicken is cut with a knife. Remove chicken pieces to individual plates. Drizzle with warm sauce. Serve chicken hot. Good with white rice and grilled pineapple.

Makes 4 servings

Chicken with Pineapple and Lichees

Fruit Sauce

2 tablespoons peanut oil
1/2 teaspoon freshly grated ginger root
3 tablespoons soy sauce
3 tablespoons dry white wine
1/2 cup canned lichees, drained
1/2 cup canned pineapple chunks, drained
1/2 cup pineapple juice
2 tablespoons cornstarch

2 tablespoons peanut oil
1/2 teaspoon freshly grated ginger root
2 chicken breasts, skin discarded, boned

Lichees are a Chinese stone fruit, slightly larger than cherries, with white flesh and an almost perfume-like taste. Canned lichees are readily available at specialty markets.

To make sauce, heat peanut oil with ginger root in a saucepan. Stir in soy sauce and white wine. Add lichees, pineapple chunks, and all but 3 tablespoons of pineapple juice. Mix reserved 3 tablespoons pineapple juice with cornstarch. Blend cornstarch mixture into sauce. Continue cooking over medium heat, stirring until the sauce thickens slightly. Set aside.

Preheat stovetop grill. Cut chicken breasts in half and then cut each piece into 4 or 5 strips. Mix oil with ginger root. Brush grill surface with flavored oil. Cook chicken strips for about 4 to 5 minutes over medium-high heat, turning once or twice during grilling. Chicken is done when it is slightly firm to the touch and juices run clear when chicken is cut with a knife.

Remove chicken strips and mound in the center of serving dish. Top with hot sauce. Serve at once. Good with rice or noodles.

Makes 4 servings

Chicken Strips
with Orange Plum Sauce

■ Brushing Spices

*1/2 teaspoon ginger
  powder*
*1 teaspoon five-spice
  powder*
1/2 teaspoon salt
1/2 cup dry white wine

*2 chicken breasts, skin
  discarded, boned*

■ Orange/Plum Sauce

*1/2 teaspoon freshly
  grated ginger root*
*2 teaspoons white
  vinegar*
1 teaspoon soy sauce
4 teaspoons sugar
*Freshly squeezed juice
  of 1 orange*
1/2 cup chicken stock
*2 tablespoons orange-
  flavored liqueur*
*2 tablespoons plum
  sauce*
*1 tablespoon cornstarch
  mixed with 2 table-
  spoons water*

*Peanut oil, for brushing
  grill*

Combine brushing spices and salt with wine.

Cut chicken breasts in half and then cut each half into 4 or 5 strips each. Brush chicken pieces generously with brushing spices. Set aside and prepare sauce.

Combine all sauce ingredients, except cornstarch mixture, in small saucepan. Bring to boil over medium heat and reduce to simmer. Stir in cornstarch mixture. Simmer until sauce thickens slightly. Reserve.

Preheat stovetop grill. Brush grill surface lightly with oil. Cook chicken strips for about 4 to 5 minutes over medium-high heat. Turn chicken strips once or twice during grilling. Chicken is done when it is slightly firm to the touch and juices run clear when chicken is cut with a knife.

Remove chicken strips and mound in the center of serving dish. Top with sauce. Serve at once. Good with rice or noodles.

Makes 4 servings

Turkey Burgers

1 pound ground turkey
2 egg whites
1/4 cup finely ground
whole wheat bread
crumbs
1 onion, minced
1/4 teaspoon each:
ground mace, salt,
and pepper

These burgers will be a favorite for guests on football weekends or aprés-ski parties. Serve with fresh cranberry relish.

To make burgers, combine ground turkey with egg whites, crumbs, onion, mace, salt, and pepper. Shape into 4 patties. Place on a plate and refrigerate until ready to grill.

Preheat grill. Cook burgers over medium-high heat, turning once. Turkey burgers will cook in about 4 minutes. Burgers will be crisp on the outside and cooked through on the inside. Remove burgers to individual dishes and serve hot. You may want to serve the burgers on warm hamburger buns.

Makes about 3 cups

Turkey Kabobs

1 pound sliced turkey breast, about 1/2 inch thick, cut in 8 strips
4 bamboo skewers, soaked in water 10 minutes, drained
8 cherry tomatoes
1 large peach, cut in quarters

1/2 cup orange juice or peach juice
1/4 cup peanut oil
1/4 teaspoon powdered ginger

Turkey is now available and plentiful throughout the year in supermarkets. You can make these turkey kabobs inside on your stovetop grill even in late fall and during the holiday season, when the markets are brimming with turkey and the prices are best.

Thread 1 tomato onto skewer, thread turkey, another tomato, and a peach quarter. Repeat until all skewers have been threaded. Place kabobs in a glass dish. Cover with orange juice mixed with oil and ginger. Let stand 1 hour. Drain and discard marinade.

Preheat stovetop grill. Cook turkey kabobs over medium-high heat for about 5 to 6 minutes or until turkey is cooked. Turn turkey as it cooks. Turkey is done when it is slightly firm to the touch. Don't overcook.

Set a kabob on each plate and spoon pickled peaches near kabob. Serve hot. Good with noodles.

Makes 4 servings

Grilled Quail with Red Seedless Grapes

4 quail, washed, patted dry, cut in half

2 cups cornmeal
1 teaspoon lemon zest
1/4 teaspoon each: salt, freshly ground black pepper, and dried marjoram
4 tablespoons ground almonds

Butter or margarine, for brushing grill

2 cups red seedless grapes

I have included this recipe as a treat to satisfy the gourmet in all of us.

Press quail flat. Mix together cornmeal, lemon zest, salt, pepper, marjoram, and ground almonds. Spread mixture on flat plate. Roll quail in the flavored cornmeal.

Preheat stovetop grill. Brush grill surface with butter. Cook quail over medium-high heat for 2 to 3 minutes per side or until done to taste. Quail should be crispy on the outside and tender on the inside. Quail is cooked when juices run clear when meat is pricked with a fork. Do not overcook.

Remove quail to a dish and decorate with grapes. Serve quail hot. Good with grilled polenta or grilled zucchini.

Makes 4 servings

SEAFOOD

Seafood provides a nearly perfect combination of taste and nutritional value. Most fish have very low levels of fat and a high protein content, making them an excellent entrée for low-cholesterol diets, weight-reduction diets, and low-sodium diets. Most fish dishes are delicate and sweet-tasting.

Some recipes in this chapter call for the grill lid to be used with the grill. This allows thicker cuts of fish, for instance fish steaks, to cook thoroughly and delicately. Cooking fish demands care and observation. Overcooking corrupts the entire concept of fish cookery and renders fish dry and tasteless. Shrimp and other shellfish become rubbery and unpleasant when overcooked.

If you catch your own fish, dress and chill your catch as quickly as you can, preferably straight from the water. Grill a fresh catch the same day, if possible. You can freeze your catch, but it is best to thaw and grill it as soon as possible.

Salmon Strips with Chopped Mint and Tomatoes

4 large ripe tomatoes, seeded and chopped
1 cup minced mint leaves
1/4 cup minced cilantro
3 green onions, minced
1/4 cup extra virgin olive oil
1/4 cup freshly squeezed lemon juice
1/4 teaspoon each: salt, pepper, and garlic powder

2 tablespoons extra virgin olive oil
1 teaspoon minced mint
1/4 teaspoon pepper

4 salmon fillets (about 6 oz each), cut in 1-inch strips

Mint is a pungent aromatic herb that grows wild throughout the world. It is very commonly found in herb gardens or as a border plant. You can generally find fresh mint in the supermarket throughout the year.

Toss tomatoes and mint together in a bowl. Blend in cilantro, onions, olive oil, lemon juice, salt, pepper, and garlic powder. Allow sauce to stand for 30 minutes at room temperature. Toss before serving. Taste to adjust seasonings.

To prepare salmon strips, mix the oil with mint and pepper. Brush salmon with flavored oil.

Preheat stovetop grill. Cook salmon strips over medium-high heat for about 4 to 5 minutes, turning after 2 minutes. Salmon is cooked when it flakes easily when prodded with a fork.

Remove salmon strips to a platter and serve immediately with chopped mint and tomatoes. Good with pasta.

Makes 4 servings

Grilled Salmon

4 salmon fillets (about 6 oz each)
2 tablespoons peanut oil

Brush salmon fillets with oil.

Preheat stovetop grill. Cook fillets over medium-high heat for about 2 to 3 minutes on each side or until fish is done to taste. Fish is done when it flakes easily when prodded with a fork. Remove salmon fillets to individual dinner plates. Serve immediately.

Makes 4 servings

Swordfish with Chive Sauce

▪ Chive Sauce

1/2 teaspoon dry
   mustard
1 1/2 tablespoons
   freshly grated ginger
1 egg yolk
2 shallots, peeled
1/4 teaspoon white
   pepper
2 teaspoons soy sauce
1/4 cup chopped chives
2 cloves garlic, peeled
Freshly squeezed juice
   of 1 lemon
3/4 cup extra virgin
   olive oil

4 swordfish steaks
   (about 6 oz each)
2 tablespoons extra
   virgin olive oil

Swordfish is dense and meaty and is usually sold as steaks. Use the grill lid for this recipe.

Tarragon, especially fresh tarragon, goes very well with fish dishes. Because it is widely used in French cooking, many French chefs grow tarragon the year around in their herb gardens. Start an indoor herb garden and it will reward you with fresh herbs throughout the year.

Blend sauce ingredients in a food processor fitted with a steel blade. With the machine running, drizzle olive oil into the bowl until all oil has been added and the sauce is well blended. Pour sauce into a bowl, cover, and refrigerate until ready to serve. Stir before serving and serve at room temperature.

Brush swordfish steaks with olive oil.

Preheat stovetop grill. Cook swordfish over medium-high heat for 2 to 3 minutes on each side or until done. Swordfish is done when it is slightly firm to the touch and flakes easily when prodded with a fork. Do not overcook or fish will be tough. You can cover with the grill lid the last 3 or 4 minutes, if desired.

Remove fish to serving dish. Spoon sauce onto 4 dinner plates. Set a piece of swordfish on the sauce. Serve hot. Good with Pineapple Cole Slaw (recipe follows).

Makes 4 servings

Pineapple Cole Slaw

6 cups shredded cabbage
1 onion, thinly sliced
1 large carrot, grated
1 cup crushed pineapple, drained

Dressing

1/2 to 3/4 cup mayonnaise
2 tablespoons sugar
2 tablespoons cider vinegar
3/4 teaspoon salt
1/2 teaspoon garlic powder
1/4 teaspoon white pepper

Place shredded cabbage in deep bowl. Toss cabbage with onion, carrot, and pineapple.

Mix mayonnaise, sugar, vinegar, salt, garlic powder, and pepper. Pour dressing over vegetables and toss well. Refrigerate overnight. Adjust seasonings to taste. Toss and serve.

Makes 6 servings

Tuna with Raspberry Sauce

■ Raspberry Sauce

1 package (10 oz) frozen raspberries, defrosted, juice included
1/2 cup sugar
2 eggs
1 egg yolk
2 tablespoons raspberry vinegar
1/4 teaspoon each: dried basil and pepper
1/2 teaspoon dried tarragon
2 cups extra virgin olive oil

2 tablespoons extra virgin olive oil
1/2 teaspoon dried tarragon
4 tuna fillets (about 6 oz each)

This recipe, unlike most of the fish recipes included here, is quite rich and a wonderful dish to serve to company.

Raspberries are considered by many to be the most elegant of all berries. The peak season for fresh raspberries is July in most areas, but they can be found from early summer to November. Fresh raspberries are highly perishable and should be used as soon as possible after they are purchased. Fresh or frozen raspberries work equally well in this recipe.

To prepare raspberry sauce, purée raspberries with the juice in a food processor fitted with a steel blade. Spoon raspberry purée into a saucepan. Stir in sugar and simmer for 10 minutes. Strain and cool.

Using the food processor, whip the eggs and egg yolk about 20 seconds. Remove the top of the processor and add vinegar, basil, pepper, and tarragon. Blend for 1 minute. Add raspberry mixture and process again for 1 minute. With the machine running, drizzle in the oil until all the oil has been added and sauce is well blended. Pour sauce into a bowl, cover, and refrigerate until serving time.

Mix the 2 tablespoons oil with tarragon. Brush tuna fillets with flavored oil. Preheat stovetop grill. Cook tuna fillets over medium-high heat, about 1 minute on each side. Cover tuna on grill with the grill lid and continue cooking for 2 to 3 minutes or until fish is done. Fish is cooked when it flakes easily when prodded with a fork.

Remove fish, place on individual plates, and drizzle with sauce. Pass remaining sauce at the table. Good with fettucine.

Makes 4 servings

Grouper Sandwich
with Horseradish Sauce

■ Onion Marinade

1 tablespoon peanut oil
1 medium onion, minced
1/2 cup beer
3 tablespoons cider vinegar
1/2 teaspoon dry mustard
1/4 teaspoon each: pepper and ground cumin

4 grouper fillets (about 6 oz each)

■ Horseradish Sauce

2 tablespoons white horseradish
1 cup low-fat, plain yogurt

2 tablespoons peanut oil
4 burger rolls, sliced
4 lettuce leaves
4 large slices tomato

Grouper is a large fish that yields excellent fillets. The meat is lean and firm and makes super sandwiches.

Although fresh grated horseradish is often available, for this recipe, I recommend using a mild, bottled horseradish sauce. Horseradish is spicy and pungent and makes a wonderful sauce for this delicious sandwich.

To prepare marinade, heat oil in saucepan. Sauté onion for 4 minutes over medium heat, stirring occasionally. Stir in remaining ingredients. Cool marinade.

Pour marinade into resealable plastic bag. Add grouper and seal bag securely. Turn bag several times, so fish is completely coated by marinade. Refrigerate and marinate for 2 hours, turning several times. Remove fish from bag and discard marinade.

Mix horseradish with yogurt and put it in a bowl.

Preheat stovetop grill. Brush grill surface lightly with peanut oil and grill grouper fillets over medium-high heat, about 2 minutes on each side or until fish is done to taste. Fish will flake easily when done.

Warm rolls, cut side down, on grill. Set a roll on each plate. Place a lettuce leaf on the open roll.

Remove grouper and set on lettuce. Top with tomato. Pass horseradish sauce at table. Good with chopped pickles.

Makes 4 servings

Orange Roughy
with Sprout Relish

■ **Sprout Relish**

1/2 pound bean sprouts
4 stalks celery, minced
1 small onion, minced
1 red bell pepper,
  chopped
1/2 cup chopped olives
1/4 cup cider vinegar
3/4 cup sugar
2 teaspoons salt
1/4 teaspoon pepper

Peanut oil, for brushing
  grill

1 1/4 pounds orange
  roughy fillets, cut into
  4 pieces

Combine relish ingredients in a deep bowl. Cover and marinate in refrigerator the day before serving. Taste to adjust seasonings and toss before serving.

Preheat stovetop grill. Brush grill surface lightly with peanut oil. Cook fish fillets over medium-high heat, 2 minutes per side or until done. Fish will flake easily when prodded with a fork and become opaque.

Remove each serving to individual plates. Serve with sprout relish.

Makes 4 servings

Orange Roughy with Chili Sauce

■ **Chili Sauce**

1 1/2 cups low-fat, plain yogurt
3 tablespoons chili sauce
3 green onions, minced

1/4 teaspoon each: ground thyme and chili powder
2 tablespoons butter or margarine, melted
1 1/4 to 1 1/2 pounds orange roughy

Combine sauce ingredients in a small bowl. Cover and refrigerate until serving time. Stir before serving.

Mix thyme and chili powder into melted butter. Brush fish with flavored butter.

Preheat stovetop grill. Grill orange roughy pieces over medium heat on both sides until fish is cooked. Do not overcook. Fish will become opaque and slightly firm to the touch. Remove roughy to individual plates. Spoon chili sauce over fish. Serve immediately.

Makes 4 servings

Catfish

1 cup evaporated milk
2 cups white cornmeal
1/2 teaspoon paprika
1/4 teaspoon each: dried
sage, dried thyme,
and pepper
4 catfish fillets (about
6 oz each)

Peanut oil, for brushing
grill surface

Pour evaporated milk into a shallow bowl.

Mix together cornmeal, paprika, sage, thyme, and pepper. Spread on a flat plate. Dip fish in milk. Drain. Roll catfish fillets in cornmeal mixture. Set catfish on a plate and refrigerate until grilling.

Preheat stovetop grill. Brush grill surface lightly with peanut oil. Cook catfish over medium-high heat for about 4 minutes or until done, turning once or twice. Fish is cooked when it flakes easily when prodded with a fork.

Remove fish and set on individual plates. Serve with sweet potato pie and salad.

Makes 4 servings

Grilled Rainbow Trout
with Parsley and Lemon Butter

■ **Parsley and Lemon Butter**

4 tablespoons butter or margarine, at room temperature
1/4 cup minced parsley
1 teaspoon lemon zest

2 rainbow trout (about 8 oz each)
2 tablespoons margarine or butter, melted
1 tablespoon peanut oil
1/4 teaspoon each: salt, pepper, garlic powder, and dried thyme
4 sprigs parsley
1 lemon, sliced thinly

Stuffing the trout with parsley sprigs and lemon slices keeps the fish moist and imparts a delightful flavor.

To make parsley and lemon butter, soften butter in a bowl, using the back of a spoon or a food processor fitted with steel blade. Mix in parsley and lemon zest. Spoon flavored butter into a small bowl or crock. Cover and set aside. Serve at room temperature.

Wash trout and pat dry with paper towels. Combine butter, oil, salt, pepper, garlic powder, and thyme. Brush fish with seasoned butter. Slide lemon slices and sprigs of parsley into the cavity of the fish.

Preheat stovetop grill. Cook trout over medium-high heat for about 1 minute on each side. Turn trout and cover with the grill lid. Continue grilling, covered, until fish is cooked, about 2 minutes longer. When done, fish will flake easily when prodded with a fork.

Place 1 trout on each plate. Serve with parsley and lemon butter and lemon slices. Good with blueberry muffins and salad.

Makes 2 servings

Blackened Redfish

■ *Blackening*
  Seasoning

1 tablespoon dried
* minced onion*
1 1/2 teaspoons cayenne
1/2 teaspoon each:
* garlic powder, dried*
* thyme, celery salt,*
* and salt*
1/4 teaspoon pepper
4 tablespoons butter or
* margarine, melted*
1 tablespoon peanut oil
4 redfish fillets (about 6
* oz each), patted dry*

This recipe for blackening seasoning can be used on many types of fish. Be sure to open your kitchen windows and turn on your stove fan while grilling this recipe.

Combine onion, cayenne, garlic powder, dried thyme, celery salt, salt, and pepper. Mix butter and peanut oil with blackening spices. Place blackening mixture into a shallow bowl.

Roll each fish fillet in the blackening mixture. Set fish on a plate and refrigerate until ready to grill.

Preheat stovetop grill. Cook fish over high heat for about 2 minutes. Make sure your kitchen is well ventilated; open a window. Turn fish over, cover with the grill lid, and continue cooking over medium-high heat for 2 to 3 minutes longer or until fish is cooked. Fish will blacken slightly on the outside and be opaque on the inside.

Remove to serving plate. Serve with Red Beans and Rice (recipe follows) and coleslaw.

Makes 4 servings

Red Beans and Rice

1 pound red beans, soaked in water overnight, drained, water reserved
1 large onion, diced
1 carrot thinly sliced
1/2 teaspoon salt
2 bay leaves
1 ham bone

2 tablespoons peanut oil
3 stalks celery, thinly sliced

1/2 teaspoon hot-pepper sauce
1/2 teaspoon salt
1/4 teaspoon cayenne

1 cup long grain rice
2 cups water
3 tablespoons peanut oil
3/4 teaspoon salt

Red beans and rice is a New Orleans favorite that can be served alone, as an entrée, or as a side dish with many foods.

Cover beans with reserved liquid and enough additional water to measure 6 cups liquid in a large pan. Add half the onion and the carrot, salt, bay leaves, and ham bone. Cover beans and simmer for 2 1/2 to 3 hours, stirring occasionally.

Heat oil in a frying pan. Sauté celery and the remaining onion until tender (about 5 minutes), stirring occasionally. Remove the ham bone from beans. Remove any ham from the bone. Stir ham and vegetables into the beans.

Remove 1 cup of the beans; purée and return to pot. Add hot-pepper sauce, salt, and cayenne. Keep warm. Discard bay leaves before serving.

Place rice and 2 cups of water, oil, and salt in a saucepan. Cover and cook over medium heat for 15 to 20 minutes.

To serve, place a scoop of rice in a shallow bowl. Ladle beans over rice. Serve hot.

Makes 6 to 8 servings

Flounder with Anise Marinade

■ Anise Marinade

1/2 cup dry white wine

1/4 cup extra virgin olive oil

1/4 teaspoon anise seeds

3 tablespoons minced parsley

4 flounder fillets (about 6 oz each)

Combine marinade ingredients in a bowl. Pour marinade into resealable plastic bag. Add flounder fillets and seal bag securely. Turn bag several times so all surfaces of fish are coated by marinade. Refrigerate and marinate for 1 hour, turning once. Drain and discard marinade.

Preheat stovetop grill. Cook flounder over medium-high heat about 4 to 5 minutes, turning once. Remove flounder to serving dish. Serve hot. Good with warm garlic bread.

Makes 4 servings

Crusted Bluefish with Grilled Endive

■ Cornmeal Coating

2 cups white cornmeal
3 tablespoons minced parsley
1/2 teaspoon dried rosemary
1/4 teaspoon dried thyme

4 bluefish fillets (about 6 oz each)
Peanut oil for brushing grill

2 tablespoons peanut oil
1/4 teaspoon dried thyme
2 heads endive, blanched, drained

The roots of endive, a member of the chicory family, can be forced to produce tightly packed white or pale yellow leaves. Although slightly bitter, this vegetable is marvelous grilled. Cut the endive in two lengthwise to grill.

Combine coating ingredients and spread mixture evenly onto a flat plate.

Roll bluefish fillets in cornmeal coating. Set fillets on a dish and refrigerate until ready to grill.

Preheat stovetop grill. Brush grill surface lightly with oil. Grill bluefish fillets over medium-high heat about 5 minutes, turning once or twice. Fish is done when it flakes easily when prodded with a fork. For best results, do not overcook. Remove fish to platter.

Mix peanut oil with thyme. Brush endive with flavored oil. Grill endive, cut side down, until golden brown, about 1 1/2 minutes. Turn once and grill a minute or longer to taste. Put endive on serving dish around bluefish and serve at once. Good with a tossed salad.

Makes 4 servings

Whitefish with Grilled Green Onions

■ Hot-Pepper Marinade

1/2 cup peanut oil
3 tablespoons freshly squeezed lime juice
1/4 teaspoon hot-pepper sauce

4 whitefish fillets (about 6 oz each)

8 green onions, trimmed

Whitefish, a member of the salmon and trout family, is common to the Great Lakes and other cold, deep fresh waters. It is generally available throughout the country.

Combine marinade ingredients in a bowl. Pour hot-pepper marinade into resealable plastic bag. Add fish and green onions. Seal bag securely. Turn bag several times so all surfaces of fish and onions are coated by marinade. Refrigerate and marinate for 1 hour, turning once. Drain whitefish. Separate onions.

Preheat grill. Cook whitefish over medium-high heat about 4 to 5 minutes, turning once. Remove each piece to an individual dish. Grill onions 1 minute on each side. Arrange 2 onions on each piece of whitefish. Serve hot. Good with lime wedges and spinach salad.

Makes 4 servings

Redfish with Red Wine Sauce

■ Red Wine Sauce

2 large shallots, minced
1 cup red wine
2 tablespoons half-and-half
8 tablespoons unsalted butter, cut into 1/2-inch chunks
1/4 teaspoon each: salt, white pepper, and dried tarragon

4 fillets redfish (about 6 oz each)
2 tablespoons peanut oil
1/4 cup minced chives, for garnish

To prepare sauce, cook shallots and red wine in a small saucepan over medium heat until liquid has been reduced to about 3 to 4 tablespoons. Strain and return liquid to saucepan. Blend in half-and-half and continue cooking over low heat until warm. Whisk in butter, a few chunks at a time. Season with salt, pepper, and tarragon.

Brush redfish fillets with peanut oil.

Preheat stovetop grill. Cook fillets over medium-high heat about 2 minutes per side or until fish is cooked, turning once. Fish is done when it flakes easily when prodded with a fork and is opaque.

Spoon sauce onto a heated plate and set redfish on top of sauce. Garnish with minced chives.

Makes 4 servings

Cod with Taramasalata

**3 thin slices white bread,
 crust removed, torn
 into quarters**
1 small onion, quartered
1 jar (4 oz) tarama
2 small cloves garlic
**3 tablespoons freshly
 squeezed lemon juice**
**1/2 cup extra virgin
 olive oil**

**2 tablespoons extra
 virgin olive oil**
**1 teaspoon freshly
 squeezed lemon juice**
**4 cod steaks or fillets,
 about 6 ounces each**

Taramasalata is a Greek sauce made from a base of tarama or cod roe. You can purchase 4-ounce jars of tarama in Greek markets or specialty food stores. In this recipe, half of the taramasalata is used as a sauce for the cod fillets; the remaining portion is used as a dip with crusty bread chunks.

To prepare taramasalata, place bread in food processor and make into crumbs. Add remaining ingredients except olive oil. Purée tarama mixture. With machine running, add oil in a slow, steady stream. Mixture should be smooth and almost light pink in color. Spoon into a crock or bowl and taste to adjust seasonings. Cover and refrigerate until serving time.

To prepare cod, mix together olive oil and juice. Brush cod fillets with mixture.

Preheat stovetop grill. Cook cod fillets over medium-high heat about 5 minutes or until done, turning fish once. Cod is cooked when it flakes easily when prodded with a fork.

Remove fish cod fillets to serving dish. Spoon taramasalata sauce on fish. Serve French bread (cut into thin slices) dipped in remaining taramasalata as a side dish with the cod fillets.

Makes 4 servings

Grilled Kippers

3 tablespoons butter or
   margarine, melted
1 tablespoon peanut oil
1/4 teaspoon pepper
2 slices red onion,
   1/2-inch thick
1 green bell pepper,
   seeded, sliced into
   1/2-inch rounds

2 smoked kippers,
   available at large fish
   markets

Kippers are actually herring that are split from head to tail, lightly brined, and then cold smoked. Wash before grilling. The grilling process here is used merely to warm the kippers. Do not overcook them.

Combine melted butter, oil, and pepper. Brush onion, pepper slices, and kippers with butter mixture.

Preheat stovetop grill. Cook onion and pepper slices over medium heat for about 1 minute on each side. Vegetables will begin to brown and be warm. Remove vegetables to a dish.

Grill smoked kippers over medium heat about 2 minutes on each side, covered with grill lid. Remember that kippers have been smoked commercially and require only heating, so do not overcook.

Remove kippers and place 1 kipper on each plate. Put onion slice and pepper rings on each kipper. Serve hot.

Makes 2 servings

Sea Scallops with Tomato and Tarragon

▣ Tomato and Tarragon Sauce

2 large, ripe tomatoes, seeded, chopped
2 tablespoons extra virgin olive oil
2 teaspoons freshly squeezed lemon juice
3 tablespoons fresh, minced tarragon
Salt and pepper to taste

2 tablespoons butter or margarine, melted
1 tablespoon extra virgin olive oil
1/4 teaspoon pepper
1 1/4 pounds sea scallops, with roe, if possible

To make sauce, place chopped tomatoes in a colander and drain for 5 minutes, then transfer to a bowl. Mix in olive oil, lemon juice, 1 tablespoon tarragon, salt, and pepper. Cover tightly and refrigerate until serving time. Just before serving, toss mixture. Taste to adjust seasonings. Spoon chopped tomatoes onto plate.

Combine melted butter with oil and pepper. Brush scallops with flavored butter.

Sprinkle remaining tarragon in the water in the drip pan of the grill. Replace stovetop grill surface. Preheat grill. Cook scallops over medium-high heat about 2 minutes on each side. Remove scallops from grill and set over tomato and tarragon sauce. Serve hot. Good with sliced cucumber and pasta shells.

Makes 4 servings

Shrimp Enchiladas

■ Sauce

3 tablespoons peanut oil
2 cloves garlic, minced
1/2 teaspoon salt
3 green onions, minced
2 to 3 jalapeño peppers, seeded and chopped (use rubber gloves)
2 cans (10 oz each) tomatillos, puréed with juice
3/4 teaspoon ground cumin
1/2 teaspoon ground oregano
2 corn tortillas, crumbled

Peanut oil, for brushing shrimp
1/2 teaspoon ground cumin

1 1/2 cups large shrimp, deveined and washed

6 flour or corn tortillas
1 large onion, cut into 6 slices

1 cup low-fat, plain yogurt
Grilled avocado slices

Tomatillos are small, green tomato-like fruits that are cooked with the skin intact. They can be found in specialty food stores. Tomatillos have a very interesting flavor hinting of lemon, apples, and herbs.

To prepare sauce, heat oil in saucepan over medium heat. Sauté garlic, salt, and onions for 4 minutes, stirring often. Mix in peppers, tomatillos, cumin, and oregano. Add tortillas. Simmer 4 to 5 minutes. Cool sauce. Purée in food processor fitted with steel blade, or use a blender. Set aside.

Mix oil with cumin. Brush shrimp with flavored oil.

Preheat stovetop grill. Cook shrimp over medium-high heat, about 3 minutes, turning once. Shrimp will turn opaque and become slightly firm. Do not overcook or they will become tough. Reserve.

Warm tortillas, one at a time, just a few seconds on each side on the grill. Grill onion slices, 1 minute per side. Remove from grill and set aside. Preheat oven to 400° F.

Arrange 1/4 cup of grilled shrimp in center of each tortilla. Place 1 slice of onion over shrimp. Top with 2 to 3 tablespoons of sauce. Roll up the tortilla and set in a flat casserole dish. Cover tortillas with remaining sauce.

Bake 10 minutes. Serve hot with yogurt and avocado slices. Good with refried beans, sliced olives, and grated cheddar cheese.

Makes 6 servings

Breaded Soft-Shelled Crabs

■ Breading

2 cups fine bread crumbs

1/2 teaspoon each: dried oregano and dried basil

1 tablespoon minced parsley

1/4 teaspoon salt

1/8 teaspoon pepper

2 tablespoons butter or margarine, melted

2 tablespoons extra virgin olive oil

8 soft-shelled crabs

Soft-shell crabs are blue crabs that have molted their shells in the process of growing new, larger shells. The crabs should be eaten on the day they are purchased.

To clean the soft-shelled crabs, place 1 crab at a time on a cutting board. Remove face portion of crab. Lift shell (it separates easily) on either side of the back. Scrape off gills. Then remove sand holder from under face area. Throw away all sections that you remove from crab. Wash the crab and dry it. Continue until all crabs have been cleaned. Having your fishmonger clean the crabs for you is the most efficient way to get the job done.

To prepare breading, mix bread crumbs with oregano, basil, parsley, salt, and pepper. Spread on a flat dish. Set aside.

Combine melted butter and olive oil and pour into a shallow bowl. Reserve.

Roll crabs in melted butter and then dust generously in bread crumbs, patting crumbs so they stick securely to the crabs.

Preheat stovetop grill. Cook crabs over medium-high heat for about 4 to 5 minutes, turning once. Crabs are cooked when the color changes from bluish to a reddish hue and they become slightly firm to the touch. Serve with your favorite potato dish and a salad. Serve 2 crabs per guest and encourage guests to eat the entire crab, including the shell.

Makes 4 servings

Mussel Packets

20 unopened mussels

1/4 cup dry white wine
2 garlic cloves, minced
1 medium onion, minced
1 medium tomato, thinly
**   sliced**

Guests will enjoy having their own individual packets of these fragrant and tasty shellfish.

For best results, buy mussels with tightly closed shells and thoroughly scrub the mussel shells before grilling.

Cut 4 sheets aluminum foil, double thickness, each large enough to hold 5 mussels in a packet. Lay foil out flat. Place mussels in center of foil. Sprinkle with white wine, garlic, onion, and tomato slices. Wrap foil around mussels and twist shut.

Preheat stovetop grill. Set mussel packets on grill surface over high heat. Cover packets with the grill lid. Cook until mussels open for about 4 to 5 minutes.

Place a mussel packet on each plate. Allow guests to open their own packet. *IMPORTANT:* Tell guests to discard any mussels that have not opened. Serve hot. Good with salad and garlic bread.

Makes 4 servings

Trout with Almonds

4 trout fillets
2 tablespoons extra
**   virgin olive oil**
Salt and pepper to taste
1/2 cup chopped al-
**   monds**

Brush trout fillets with oil and sprinkle with salt and pepper.

Preheat stovetop grill. Cook trout over medium heat, turning once. Fish is done when it flakes easily when prodded with a fork. Place fish on individual dinner plates and sprinkle with almonds. Serve hot.

Makes 4 servings

VEGETABLES

- Ideally, vegetables should be picked fresh from the garden, prepared immediately after picking, and cooked to perfection. Too often, however, vegetables are cooked to death, destroying their natural flavors and textures. Vegetables should never be over-cooked. The stovetop grill works masterfully with vegetable dishes. The intense heat of the grill cooks virtually any vegetable quickly and thoroughly while retaining both flavor and the desired degree of crunchiness.

- Thick vegetables, such as potatoes, carrots, and whole onions, should be sliced before grilling. Thicker vegetables should be boiled or blanched before being grilled. The grill will enhance the flavor and texture of precooked vegetables.

- During the summer and fall, you can make good use of the fresh bounty of the garden. During winter and early spring, you can enjoy the thrill of the grill with frozen vegetables and fill your kitchen with the aroma of grilling vegetables, regardless of the weather outside.

Corn on the Cob
with Blue Cheese Butter

4 fresh ears of corn

■ **Blue Cheese Butter**

4 tablespoons butter or margarine, at room temperature
3 ounces crumbled blue cheese
1/4 teaspoon Dijon mustard

This recipe gives a unique and tangy approach to corn on the cob. Using corn immediately after picking ensures the sweetest and freshest flavor. If you are buying corn from a vegetable stand or at a farmer's market, ask for ears that have been picked the same day you purchase them.

A blue cheese fanatic, I find that blue cheese has a bite and flavor that adds zest to many dishes.

Pull husks back from corn. Remove silk. Replace outer husks. Cover ears with water and soak in husks for 10 minutes. Drain.

Meanwhile, prepare blue cheese butter. Soften butter in a bowl, using the back of a spoon or use a food processor fitted with steel blade. Mix in blue cheese and Dijon mustard. Spoon flavored butter into a bowl or crock.

Again pull back outer husks and brush corn liberally with blue cheese butter.

Preheat stovetop grill. Grill corn over medium heat about 3 minutes, rotating after each minute. Corn husks will char slightly, but corn will be tender and warm. Remove to serving dish and serve hot. You may want to serve additional blue cheese butter with the hot corn.

Makes 4 servings

Eggplant Parmigiana on the Grill

1 medium eggplant, peeled
Salt

1/2 teaspoon dried oregano
Extra virgin olive oil, for brushing eggplant slices

8 tablespoons tomato sauce
4 slices mozzarella cheese, cut slightly smaller than each eggplant slice
1/4 cup freshly grated Parmesan cheese
1 tablespoon minced parsley

Eggplant is available in most produce departments throughout the year, although the vegetable is most plentiful in the late summer and early fall. Eggplant retains a good deal of moisture; to remove excess moisture, salt and drain eggplant slices on a rack before grilling. Eggplant discolors rapidly but will retain a fresh look if sprinkled with lemon juice. Choose eggplant that is firm and heavy, with a dark, shiny, smooth skin.

Parmesan is an Italian hard cheese that imparts a strong, fragrant quality to this dish.

Cut eggplant into 1/2-inch slices. Spread eggplant slices on paper towels. Sprinkle with salt and let stand for 40 minutes. Wash off salt and pat eggplant dry with paper towels.

Preheat stovetop grill. Mix oregano with olive oil. Brush eggplant slices with flavored oil. Grill eggplant over medium-high heat, 1 1/2 to 2 minutes per side.

While eggplant is still on the grill, spread 2 tablespoons tomato sauce on each eggplant slice, using the back of a spoon. Layer a slice of mozzarella cheese on each eggplant slice. Sprinkle with Parmesan cheese. Continue grilling another 1 to 2 minutes. Mozzarella will begin to melt around edges, and eggplant will be cooked through.

Remove eggplant slices to serving dish. Sprinkle with parsley and serve immediately.

Makes 4 servings

Grilled Eggplant Slices with Parsley Sauce

1 eggplant
Salt

■ Parsley Sauce

1 small boiled potato
**2 tablespoons freshly
squeezed lemon juice**
2 cloves garlic, minced
**3 anchovy fillets,
drained**
1/4 cup chopped parsley
2 teaspoons capers
1/4 teaspoon pepper
**1/4 cup plus 3 table-
spoons extra virgin
olive oil**

**1/2 teaspoon dried
oregano**

Cut eggplant into 1/2-inch slices.

Spread the eggplant slices on paper towels and sprinkle with salt. Let eggplant slices stand for 40 minutes. Wash off salt and pat slices dry with paper towels.

Peel potato and cut in half.

Using a food processor fitted with steel blade, puree all sauce ingredients except olive oil. With the machine running, pour 1/4 cup olive oil through the food tube until ingredients are blended. Pour sauce into a bowl, cover, and refrigerate.

Mix 3 tablespoons olive oil with oregano. Brush eggplant slices with flavored oil.

Preheat stovetop grill. Cook eggplant slices over medium-high heat about 2 minutes on each side. Eggplant should be a golden brown on the outside and tender on the inside. Remove eggplant slices to serving dish. Drizzle with parsley sauce. Serve hot.

Makes 4 servings

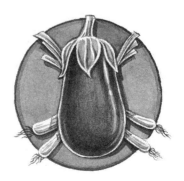

Avocado Slices

1 large ripe avocado
3 tablespoons freshly squeezed lime juice

Butter or margarine, melted, to brush avocado

4 lettuce leaves

1 can (4 oz) mild green chiles, drained, seeded
2 tablespoons minced cilantro

Avocados are native to America and are rich in vitamins. While avocados are best known as the soul of guacamole, these grilled avocado slices make a delicious, creative addition to a meal.

Peel avocado, discard pit, and slice. Sprinkle avocado with lime juice.

Preheat stovetop grill. Brush avocado slices with butter. Grill avocado slices over medium-high heat for 1 minute per side. Avocado will be warm on the inside and lightly browned on the outside.

Arrange a lettuce leaf on each salad plate. Arrange avocado slices over lettuce. Sprinkle with chiles and cilantro. Serve warm.

Makes 4 servings

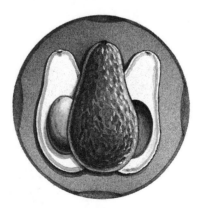

Parsnips and Pears

4 firm, ripe pears
6 medium parsnips
2 tablespoons dark brown sugar
1/8 teaspoon ground cinnamon
3 tablespoons butter or margarine, melted

Parsnips are available year-round in produce departments, but they are most plentiful in fall and winter. Buy small- to medium-sized parsnips that are firm and well-shaped. Avoid large, woody parsnips or any with blemishes or dried-up roots.

This recipe combines parsnips and pears to yield an interesting blend of flavors and textures.

Peel pears and cut into quarters. Discard seeds.

Peel parsnips and cut each into 4 chunks. Cover parsnips with water and cook until just fork tender. Drain and cool.

Mix brown sugar and cinnamon into melted butter.

Preheat stovetop grill. Brush parsnip and pear pieces with melted butter. Grill parsnip and pear pieces over medium-high heat, turning once or twice, until both are warm and tender, about 2 to 3 minutes.

Remove parsnip and pear pieces to serving dish. Serve hot.

Makes 6 servings

Leeks with Tomatoes and Basil

■ Basil Butter

4 tablespoons butter or margarine, at room temperature
1 tablespoon minced fresh basil

4 medium-sized leeks, trimmed
Extra virgin olive oil, for brushing leeks
1 clove garlic, minced
1 tablespoon freshly squeezed lemon juice

2 large tomatoes, sliced
2 tablespoons minced parsley
Salt, pepper, and dried oregano to taste

Leeks possess a faint onion taste, although they are much milder and sweeter. Look for leeks that are evenly shaped and straight, with a white base. The white portion of the leek is used in cooking; the top green leaves are discarded. Leeks tend to be sandy, so wash them well.

Basil is a natural complement to tomatoes. If possible, use freshly picked basil, which has an intense, sweet smell.

To prepare basil butter, soften butter in a bowl, using the back of a spoon or use a food processor fitted with steel blade. Mix in basil. Set aside.

Cut leeks in half horizontally and brush with olive oil.

Preheat stovetop grill. Grill leeks over medium heat, cut side down, for 2 minutes. Turn leeks over and continue grilling for 1 to 2 minutes. Leeks should char slightly and be fork tender. Remove leeks to a serving dish. Sprinkle with garlic and lemon juice.

Surround leeks with sliced tomatoes. Dot leeks with basil butter. Sprinkle with parsley. Season to taste with salt, pepper, and oregano. Serve hot.

Makes 4 servings

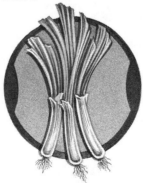

Cherry Tomato Kabobs
with Chive Butter

■ **Chive Butter**

4 tablespoons butter or margarine, room temperature
2 teaspoons minced chives
1/2 teaspoon dried tarragon

16 cherry tomatoes, blossoms removed
4 8-inch bamboo skewers, soaked in water 10 minutes, drained
Peanut oil, for brushing grill

To prepare chive butter, mix softened butter with chives and tarragon, using the back of a spoon, or use a mini food processor. Spoon chive butter into a small bowl. Cover and set aside.

Thread tomatoes onto skewers.

Preheat stovetop grill. Brush grill surface lightly with peanut oil. Cook skewered tomatoes over medium heat about 1 to 2 minutes, turning often. Tomatoes will begin to blister and brown. Do not let tomatoes overcook and become soggy. Remove to serving dish.

Spoon chive butter over tomatoes and serve hot.

Makes 4 servings

Red Onion Slices with Bacon

2 slices lean bacon, cut in half
1 large red onion
2 tablespoons minced parsley

Preheat stovetop grill. Cook bacon strips over medium-high heat until brown and crisp, turning as needed. Drain on paper towels.

Cut onion into thin slices, set aside.

Grill red onion without cleaning grill surface, 1 minute on each side. Place onions on serving dish. Crumble bacon over onion and sprinkle with parsley. Serve hot.

Makes 4 servings

Leeks and Shallots
with Hazelnut Butter

■ Hazelnut Butter

**4 tablespoons butter or
margarine, at room
temperature**
**2 tablespoons ground
hazelnuts or peanuts**
**1/4 teaspoon dried
tarragon**

**4 medium-sized leeks,
trimmed**
**4 large shallots, thinly
sliced horizontally**
**1 tablespoon butter or
margarine, for
brushing shallots
and leeks**
Salt and pepper to taste

Shallots are milder in taste than their cousin, the onion. They tend to have a slight garlic flavor and, like garlic, have small bulbs that can be separated into cloves.

Hazelnuts are frequently used in dessert recipes, but their delicious flavor contributes a richness to many nondessert foods as well. Leeks tend to be sandy, so wash carefully.

Soften butter in a bowl, using the back of a spoon or use a food processor fitted with steel blade. Mix in hazelnuts and tarragon. Remove flavored butter to a bowl. Set aside.

Cut leeks in half horizontally. Slice shallots thinly.

Preheat stovetop grill. Brush leeks with melted butter. Grill over medium-high heat, cut side down, for 2 minutes. Turn leeks over and continue grilling for 1 to 2 minutes. Leeks should char slightly and be fork tender. Remove leeks to serving dish. Dot with hazelnut butter.

Grill shallots quickly, about 1 minute per side. Brush shallots with butter as they cook, turning frequently until they soften. Sprinkle shallots over leeks.

Dot with hazelnut butter and serve hot.

Makes 4 servings

Fennel

4 fennel bulbs
1 tablespoon caraway
seeds
2 tablespoons butter or
margarine, melted
4 tablespoons freshly
grated Parmesan
cheese

Fennel is native to southern Europe, but is now commonly cultivated in the United States. This vegetable has a mild licorice (anise) flavor. In fact, oil of fennel makes up 90 percent of the essential oil in anise.

Fennel makes a wonderful accompaniment to fish and pork. The freshest bulbs of fennel are well-rounded and pale green to white in color. Deep green bulbs are over-ripe.

Trim fennel bulbs and cut into 1/2- to 1/4-inch slices. Cover fennel with salted water in saucepan. Bring to a boil over medium heat. Reduce heat to simmer. Continue cooking, uncovered, until fennel slices are fork tender, about 6 to 8 minutes. Drain and cool.

Mix caraway seeds into butter and brush fennel slices. Preheat stovetop grill. Cook fennel slices over medium-high heat for about 1 minute on each side. Fennel will brown slightly on the outside and be tender on the inside.

Remove fennel slices to serving dish. Sprinkle with freshly grated Parmesan cheese and serve hot.

Makes 4 servings

Green Tomatoes

3/4 cup cornmeal
1/4 teaspoon each:
    garlic powder and
    dried sage
Salt and pepper to taste
3 large green tomatoes,
    cut into 1/2-inch slices

Peanut oil, for brushing
    grill
2 tablespoons minced
    parsley

Green tomatoes are excellent when grilled. This recipe is good for the fall bounty of green tomatoes.

Mix cornmeal with garlic, sage, salt, and pepper. Spread on a flat plate. Dust both sides of green tomato slices with flavored cornmeal.

Preheat stovetop grill. Brush grill surface lightly with oil. Cook tomato slices over medium-high heat about 1 to 2 minutes per side. Turn tomatoes once during grilling. Tomatoes will be crusty on the outside and warm on the inside.

Remove tomato slices to serving plate. Sprinkle with minced parsley. Serve tomato slices hot.

Make 4 servings

Red Pepper Strips with Tomato Concasse

■ Tomato Concasse

2 pounds ripe tomatoes
1/2 teaspoon each: salt and dried basil
1/4 teaspoon pepper

4 large red bell peppers

Red bell peppers are not hot; they have a mild, sweet taste. While this recipe calls for red peppers, you can use green or yellow bell peppers with equal success. Bell peppers can be stored in the refrigerator but will hold their freshness and texture only a few days. Choose bright-colored, firm, well-shaped bell peppers.

To prepare Tomato Concasse, peel, seed, and roughly chop tomatoes. Put tomatoes in colander or sieve, and let drain 5 minutes. Remove tomatoes to bowl and sprinkle with salt and basil. Cover and refrigerate until needed. Stir before placing over peppers.

Preheat stovetop grill. Cook peppers over high heat until charred on all sides. Using a fork, transfer the peppers to a plastic bag. Close the bag and let the peppers stand for 20 minutes. Remover peppers from the bag. Peel off the skin; discard stems and seeds.

Slice peppers into thin strips. Arrange peppers decoratively on a plate. Top with Tomato Concasse.

Makes 4 servings

Artichoke and Mushroom Kabobs

Marinade

Juice of 1/2 lemon or lime
4 tablespoons extra virgin olive oil
1 tablespoon dried basil
1/2 teaspoon garlic powder
2 bay leaves

1 can (14 1/2 oz) artichoke hearts, drained
12 medium mushrooms, cleaned and trimmed
4 bamboo skewers, soaked in water 10 minutes, drained

It has been said that "eating an artichoke is like getting to know someone really well." The edible parts of the leaves of the artichoke are the fleshy bottoms of the leaves and the base beneath the "choke."

Combine marinade ingredients in bowl. Pour marinade into resealable plastic bag. Add artichokes and mushrooms. Seal bag securely. Turn bag several times so marinade coats all the vegetables. Refrigerate and marinate for 2 hours. Drain and discard marinade.

Thread artichokes and mushrooms alternately onto skewers.

Preheat stovetop grill. Grill vegetable kabobs over medium heat for 3 to 4 minutes, turning every minute or as necessary. Cook until vegetables are tender, or to taste. Vegetables should begin to brown on the outside and be tender on the inside.

Remove kabobs from grill, set decoratively on platter, and serve on a buffet or pass at the table. Serve kabobs hot or at room temperature.

Makes 4 servings

Plantains

**3 large, ripe plantains
3 tablespoons minced
   cilantro, divided
2 tablespoons butter or
   margarine, melted
Salt to taste**

Plantains are available in specialty markets or large supermarkets. They are similar in shape and size to a banana but are not as sweet. They retain a green color when ripe. Plantains must be cooked before eating.

Peel and cut plantains into 1/2-inch pieces. Press plantain slices with a spatula. Put plantain slices on a dish and set aside.

Mix 1/2 tablespoon of cilantro with melted butter. Brush plantain slices with flavored butter.

Preheat stovetop grill. Cook plantain slices over medium heat about 1 minute on each side. Plantains should be a golden brown outside and tender and warm inside. Remove plantain slices to serving dish.

Sprinkle with salt and remaining cilantro. Serve hot. Good as an appetizer or a vegetable course.

Makes 4 to 6 servings

Acorn Squash with Brown Sugar

**2 acorn squash, cut in
half, seeds removed
2 tablespoons butter or
margarine, melted
1/4 cup firmly packed
dark brown sugar
1/4 teaspoon each: salt,
pepper, and ground
cinnamon
1/2 cup chopped
walnuts**

Cover acorn squash halves with cold water in a large saucepan. Bring to a boil over medium heat and continue cooking for 20 minutes or until the squash are just fork tender, yet firm. Drain and cool. Peel squash and cut into 1/2-inch rings.

Mix melted butter with sugar, salt, pepper, and ground cinnamon. Brush squash rings with flavored butter.

Preheat stovetop grill. Grill squash rings over medium heat for 1 minute on each side. Squash will begin to brown on each side. Place on serving plate and sprinkle with walnuts. Serve hot.

Makes 4 servings

Zucchini with Tomato Sauce

■ Tomato Sauce

**2 tablespoons extra
    virgin olive oil
2 cloves garlic, minced
1 onion, minced
1/2 pound ground beef
1 can (28 oz) tomatoes,
    with juice
1 can (6 oz) tomato
    paste
2 bay leaves
3/4 teaspoon dried basil
1/2 teaspoon each: dried
    oregano and salt
1/4 teaspoon freshly
    ground pepper**

**3 small zucchini (ap-
    proximately 4 inches
    long)
1/4 teaspoon each:
    garlic powder, salt,
    and pepper
Extra virgin olive oil, for
    brushing zucchini**

To prepare tomato sauce, heat olive oil in frying pan over medium heat. Sauté garlic and onion for 4 minutes, stirring occasionally. Mix in ground beef and cook until meat is just browned, about 10 minutes. Add tomatoes and juice, tomato paste, bay leaves, basil, oregano, salt, and pepper. Simmer uncovered until sauce thickens, about 45 minutes, stirring occasionally. Discard bay leaves.

Cut zucchini in half horizontally.

To prepare zucchini, mix garlic powder, salt, and pepper into olive oil. Brush zucchini with flavored oil.

Preheat stovetop grill. Cook zucchini, cut side down, over medium heat for 1 1/2 minutes. Brush zucchini again with flavored oil and turn. Grill for 1 to 2 minutes or until zucchini are cooked to taste. Zucchini should be fork tender. Remove zucchini to serving plate. Cover with tomato sauce. Serve hot.

VARIATION: Grill zucchini as above, but serve sprinkled with 1/2 cup slivered almonds instead of tomato sauce.

Makes 4 servings

Chanterelle Mushrooms

**1 pound chanterelle
  mushrooms
2 tablespoons butter or
  margarine, melted
1 tablespoon peanut oil
1/4 teaspoon each: dried
  tarragon and pepper
1/4 cup minced parsley**

Chanterelles are dainty, trumpet-shaped, reddish-golden wild mushrooms. They have a somewhat nutty, slightly apricot taste.

Warning: Never eat or cook with a wild mushroom that hasn't been properly identified. Chanterelles are available in large supermarkets, although regular button mushrooms can be substituted.

Trim, wash, and pat chanterelle mushrooms dry with paper towels.

Mix melted butter and peanut oil together with dried tarragon and pepper. Brush mushrooms with flavored butter.

Preheat stovetop grill. Cook mushrooms over medium heat, in a single layer, for about 2 to 3 minutes. Turn mushrooms as needed. Mushrooms should be warm and a golden brown. Remove to serving dish. Serve mushrooms hot, sprinkled with parsley.

Makes 4 servings

Polenta with Tomato Sauce

Olive oil, for coating pan
4 cups water
2 teaspoons salt
1/2 cups yellow
cornmeal
2 tablespoons butter or
margarine, melted

■ **Tomato Sauce**

4 large tomatoes,
chopped
1/2 cup chopped celery
1 red bell pepper,
seeded, chopped
1/2 teaspoon each: dried
basil and salt
1/2 teaspoon prepared
mustard
1/4 cup sugar
1/4 cup cider vinegar

2 tablespoons extra
virgin olive oil, for
brushing polenta

Polenta is prepared with coarse yellow corn meal and can be served as a main dish or as a vegetable. I like to prepare polenta in the classic style and then grill it.

Coat loaf pan with olive oil.

Bring salted water to a boil over high heat. Add cornmeal in a slow, steady stream, stirring constantly with a wooden spoon to press out lumps. Stir until all cornmeal has been added. Simmer and stir continuously for 45 minutes. Mixture should be thick and pull away from sides of pan. Mix in butter.

Pour polenta into prepared loaf pan. Refrigerate until set, about 1 hour. Remove polenta from pan and cut into 1/2-inch slices.

While polenta is chilling, prepare tomato sauce. Combine tomatoes, celery, and pepper in a deep bowl. In a small bowl, combine basil, salt, mustard, sugar, and vinegar. Toss to combine ingredients. Cover and refrigerate until needed. Adjust seasonings to taste and toss before serving.

Preheat stovetop grill. Brush 6 polenta slices with oil. Cook polenta over medium-high heat for 2 minutes per side. Polenta should brown slightly on outside and be warm inside. Serve polenta hot with tomato sauce.

Makes 4 to 6 servings

Polenta with Sage

Olive oil, for coating loaf pan

4 cups water
2 teaspoons salt
1/2 cups yellow cornmeal
1/2 teaspoon dried sage or 1 teaspoon fresh sage
2 tablespoons butter or margarine, melted

2 tablespoons extra virgin olive oil
1/2 teaspoon dried sage

Coat loaf pan with olive oil.

Bring salted water to a boil over high heat. Add cornmeal in a slow, steady stream, stirring constantly with a wooden spoon to press out lumps. Stir until all cornmeal has been added. Stir in sage, reduce heat to low, and cook for 45 minutes, stirring frequently. Mixture should be thick and pull away from sides of pan. Mix in butter.

Pour polenta into prepared loaf pan. Refrigerate until set, about 1 hour. Remove polenta from pan. Cut into 1/2-inch slices.

Preheat stovetop grill. Blend olive oil and sage together. Brush polenta slices with oil mixture. Cook polenta over medium-high heat for 2 minutes per side or until polenta is just browned outside and warm inside. Serve hot.

Makes 4 servings

Garlic Potatoes

4 large potatoes, peeled
4 tablespoons butter or
margarine, melted
1/2 teaspoon each:
garlic powder and
dried oregano

Bring salted water to a boil over high heat and add potatoes. Cook over medium heat until potatoes are just fork tender. Drain and cool. Slice each potato horizontally into 6 wedges.

Mix melted butter with garlic powder and oregano. Brush potatoes with flavored butter.

Preheat grill. Cook potatoes over medium-high heat about 3 minutes. Turn potatoes so all sides will brown slightly. Remove potatoes to serving dish. Serve hot.

Makes 4 servings

Sweet Potato Chips

3 large sweet potatoes

3 tablespoons butter or
margarine, melted
1 tablespoon peanut oil
1/2 teaspoon garlic
powder
1/4 teaspoon ground
nutmeg
Salt to taste

Peel sweet potatoes and cut in half crosswise. Cover potatoes with salted water in a large saucepan. Bring to boil, reduce heat, and cook over medium heat for 15 to 20 minutes or until potatoes are fork tender but still firm. Drain potatoes and cool.

Slice potatoes in 1/4- to 1/2-inch slices and set on a plate. Mix melted butter and oil with garlic powder and nutmeg. Brush potatoes with flavored butter.

Preheat stovetop grill. Cook sweet potato slices over medium-high heat until potatoes are warm on the inside and crisp on the outside (about 1 minute per side). Remove to serving dish and sprinkle with salt. Serve hot.

Makes 4 servings

Potatoes Italienne

1 pound small red (new)
potatoes
Salt

2 tablespoons extra
virgin olive oil
2 cloves garlic, minced
1 teaspoon dried
oregano
1/2 tablespoons minced
parsley
3 tomatoes, chopped
Salt and pepper to taste

2 tablespoons butter or
margarine, melted
2 tablespoons peanut oil

This potato dish is enhanced by two popular, flavorful herbs: oregano and parsley. Oregano is widely used in Italian dishes, particularly those with tomato and cheese. Dried oregano imparts a strong and pungent flavor to this potato dish.

Parsley makes a fine window box or potted plant. It can be grown year-round and used for flavoring or as a garnish with a wide variety of dishes.

Cover potatoes with salted water in large pan. Bring to a boil, reduce heat to medium, and continue cooking until potatoes are done but still firm. Cool. Peel potatoes and cut into 1/4-inch-thick slices.

While potatoes are cooking, heat oil in a frying pan. Sauté garlic for 1 minute. Stir in oregano, parsley, and tomatoes. Season with salt and pepper to taste. Simmer for 5 to 6 minutes, stirring occasionally. Remove from heat. Pour mixture over potato slices.

Preheat stovetop grill. Mix butter and peanut oil together and brush potato slices with oil mixture. Cook over medium-high heat until crispy on the outside and warm on the inside for about 1 to 2 minutes. Turn potatoes once during grilling; brush with oil during turning. Place potatoes in serving bowl.

Makes 4 servings

Red Cabbage with Grilled Apple Rings

2 Granny Smith apples

*4 tablespoons butter or
  margarine*
*1 medium head red
  cabbage, shredded*
1/2 teaspoon salt
*1/4 teaspoon each:
  ground nutmeg and
  ground pepper*
*5 tablespoons white
  vinegar*
*5 tablespoons dark
  brown sugar*
1/2 cup dark raisins

■ *Apple Rings*

*2 tablespoons butter or
  margarine, melted*
1 tablespoon peanut oil
*1/2 teaspoon grated
  lemon zest*
*2 large Granny Smith
  apples*

To prepare cabbage, first peel, core, and chop the two apples. Heat butter in a large heavy saucepan. Add cabbage and apples. Sprinkle with salt, nutmeg, pepper, vinegar, sugar, and raisins. Cook over medium heat, covered, for 35 minutes, stirring occasionally. Check mixture after 10 minutes. If it is too dry, add 1/2 cup water or water as needed.

To prepare apple rings, first peel and core the two apples, then cut into 1/2-inch rounds. Preheat grill. Mix butter, oil, and lemon zest together. Brush apple slices with butter mixture. Cook apple rings over medium-high heat for 1 minute on each side. Apples should be golden brown outside and still firm inside.

Spoon hot cooked cabbage mixture into serving dish. Arrange apple rings decoratively over top. Serve hot.

Makes 4 servings

DESSERTS

■ Desserts and the stovetop grill are a natural if surprising combination. The results can be both rewarding and heart-warming, the perfect conclusion to many meals.

■ Fruit is a refreshing dessert and works especially well on the grill. You can achieve many delectable combinations of warm grilled fruits and cheeses. Liqueur flavorings and sauces also go well with most grilled fruits. One of my all-time favorite desserts is grilled pineapple slices, either served alone or covered with warm cheese.

Pineapple Slices over Pineapple Sherbet

1 fresh pineapple, crown discarded, peeled

1 tablespoon honey
3 tablespoons butter or margarine, melted

4 scoops pineapple sherbet

Slice pineapple into 1/2-inch rounds.

Combine honey and melted butter in a small bowl.

Preheat stovetop grill over medium-high heat. Brush pineapple slices with honey mixture. Grill pineapple about 1 1/2 minutes per side.

Quickly arrange pineapple slices on dessert dishes. Place a scoop of pineapple sherbet in center of dish. Serve at once. Good with cookies.

Makes 4 servings

Fruit Kabobs
with Warm Pound Cake

Raspberry Sauce

1 package (10 oz) raspberries, defrosted, juice included
2 teaspoons freshly squeezed lime juice
1/4 cup sugar

6 8-inch bamboo skewers, soaked in water 10 minutes, drained
1 can (5 1/2 oz) pineapple chunks, drained
2 bananas, cut into 1-inch pieces
3 1-inch thick slices pound cake

4 tablespoons melted margarine or butter
1 tablespoon dark rum, optional

Fruit kabobs are an often overlooked grilled dish that can be used as a sweet salad or as a dessert.

Cut pound cake into 1-inch cubes.

To prepare sauce, purée raspberries in a food processor fitted with steel blade or use a blender. Combine lime juice and sugar with raspberries in a small saucepan. Simmer for 3 to 4 minutes. Strain sauce and discard seeds. Set aside.

Thread skewers with pineapple chunks, bananas, and pound cake.

Mix butter and rum together. Brush kabobs with butter mixture. Preheat stovetop grill. Cook kabobs over medium-high heat, just until hot. Turn kabobs often, brushing them as you turn. Remove from grill.

Spoon raspberry sauce into individual dishes. Set kabobs on sauce. Serve immediately.

Makes 6 servings

Strawberries over Strawberry Ice Cream

■ Hot Fudge Sauce

3/4 cup good-quality cocoa
1 cup sugar
1 cup evaporated milk
1/2 cup light corn syrup
1/2 cup butter or margarine
1 1/2 teaspoons vanilla

20 large, firm strawberries, washed, hulls intact
4 bamboo skewers, soaked in water 10 minutes, drained
4 double scoops strawberry ice cream

To make hot fudge sauce, mix cocoa and sugar in a saucepan. Mix in milk and corn syrup. Simmer, stirring often, until sauce comes to a boil. Continue cooking, stirring constantly, for 30 seconds. Remove syrup from heat. Whisk in butter and vanilla. Serve sauce warm.

Thread strawberries on skewers. Preheat stovetop grill. Cook berries over medium heat, just to warm them, about 30 seconds on each side. Do not let berries become mushy.

To serve, divide ice cream among 4 sauce dishes. Ladle hot fudge sauce over ice cream. Set warm strawberries on top of ice cream. Serve immediately.

Makes 4 servings

Orange Slices with Blueberries

**4 large navel oranges,
peeled**
**1 cup plus 2 tablespoons
dry sherry, divided**
1 pint blueberries
**3 tablespoons light
brown sugar**
**2 tablespoons butter or
margarine**

Peel oranges and cut into 1/4-inch slices. Place orange slices in bowl. Sprinkle half of sherry over oranges. Let stand at room temperature for 1 hour, turning once. Drain.

Meanwhile pick over blueberries, discarding any bruised berries. Wash; drain on paper towels.

Toss berries with remainder of sherry. Set aside.

Preheat stovetop grill. Mix sugar and butter together. Brush grill surface with sweetened butter. Grill orange slices over medium heat, 1 minute on each side. Set warm orange slices on dessert dishes. Sprinkle with blueberries and serve immediately.

Makes 4 servings

Papaya with Blueberries

**2 cups low-fat vanilla
   yogurt**
**1/3 cup firmly packed
   light brown sugar**
3 tablespoons dark rum

**1 papaya (enough for 4
   servings)**
**4 tablespoons butter or
   margarine**
**1 pint fresh or defrosted
   frozen blueberries**

Fresh blueberries are ideal in this recipe, but frozen, defrosted berries will also work well.

Golden brown papaya slices are wonderful served fresh from the grill. The blueberries give this dessert a pleasing color combination.

Mix yogurt, sugar, and rum together. Spoon into a bowl. Refrigerate until serving time.

Peel and seed the papaya before cutting it into 3/4-inch spears. Brush papaya with butter. Preheat stovetop grill. Cook papaya over medium heat, about 1 to 1 1/2 minutes on each side. Remove to serving dish. Serve immediately with blueberries and vanilla yogurt mixture.

Makes 4 servings

Fruit Salad with Grilled Brie

1 medium cantaloupe
1/2 honeydew
4 lettuce leaves
2 cups watermelon cubes
1/2 pound seedless green
    or red grapes, cut in
    small bunches
4 ounces Brie cheese
1 cup lemon yogurt
1/2 cup slivered almonds

To me, Brie is truly one of the world's greatest, most exquisite cheeses. It is a natural for the grill.

Cut cantaloupe and honeydew into wedges; peel and discard seeds.

Arrange lettuce leaves on each plate. Divide and arrange cantaloupe and honeydew decoratively on lettuce. Place watermelon and grapes around lettuce.

Cut Brie into 4 portions. Preheat stovetop grill. Cook Brie over medium heat for about 30 seconds on each side. Brie should be just warm and almost runny.

Remove cheese from grill and set on fruit plates. Spoon a dollop of lemon yogurt in center of fruit plates and sprinkle with almonds. Eat at once.

Makes 4 servings

S'Mores

3 chocolate bars (5 oz each)
8 squares graham crackers
8 large marshmallows

S'Mores are one of the great delights of childhood. But don't forget that adults love them too!

Set half a chocolate bar on 1 graham cracker. Place 2 marshmallows in center over chocolate. Press remaining graham cracker into place, forming the famous graham cracker sandwich called a S'More. Wrap each S'More in aluminum foil.

Preheat stovetop grill. Cook S'Mores over medium-high heat for 1 minute on each side. Serve immediately.

Makes 4 servings

Bananas Foster

3 tablespoons butter or margarine, melted
1 teaspoon peanut oil
3 tablespoons light brown sugar
1/4 teaspoon ground cinnamon
1/8 teaspoon ground nutmeg

4 large firm bananas, cut in half horizontally

4 double scoops vanilla ice cream

Bananas Foster was created and popularized at Brennan's Restaurant in New Orleans during the 1950s. Today it is a favorite dessert throughout the country.

Mix melted butter with peanut oil, brown sugar, cinnamon, and nutmeg. Brush bananas with flavored butter mixture.

Preheat stovetop grill. Cook bananas over medium-high heat for 1 minute on each side. To serve, set ice cream in 4 dishes. Quickly set bananas over ice cream. Serve immediately.

Makes 4 servings

Peaches with Bourbon Sauce

■ Bourbon Sauce

**1 cup heavy cream or
  half-and-half
1/4 cup sugar
4 egg yolks
1/8 teaspoon ground
  nutmeg
1/4 cup Bourbon**

**4 ripe peaches
Butter or margarine,
  melted, for brushing
  peaches**

To make sauce, mix cream and sugar together in a small sauce-pan. Simmer, stirring constantly, until sugar has melted. Remove mixture from heat and cool.

Beat egg yolks with nutmeg until light. In a slow, steady stream, add cream mixture, beating to blend ingredients.

Pour sauce in top pan of a double boiler over simmering water. Simmer for 5 minutes, stirring often. Mixture will thicken slightly.

Pour sauce into a bowl, stir in Bourbon, cover, and chill until ready to serve.

Blanch peaches and peel off skins. Cut peaches in half and discard stones. Brush with butter.

Preheat stovetop grill. Cook peaches over medium heat, cut side down, for 2 minutes. Turn over and grill for 1 minute over medium-high heat. Remove peaches to individual serving dishes. Pass Bourbon Sauce at table, allowing guests to help themselves. Good with cookies.

Makes 4 servings

Pears with Coffee Liqueur Sauce

■ **Coffee Liqueur Sauce**

1 cup small curd cottage cheese
1 cup non-dairy whipped cream
1/2 cup light brown sugar
1 cup vanilla yogurt
1/3 cup coffee-flavored liqueur
1/2 teaspoon ground cinnamon

2 tablespoons butter or margarine, melted
1 teaspoon peanut oil
1/4 teaspoon ground cinnamon
2 tablespoons sugar
4 ripe pears, quartered, cored

This recipe is an interesting combination of tastes. The coffee sauce features yogurt and coffee liqueur.

To make sauce, purée cottage cheese in food processor fitted with steel blade. Remove cheese and place in a bowl. Blend in whipped cream, sugar, yogurt, liqueur, and cinnamon. Cover and refrigerate until ready to serve. Sauce can be prepared the day before serving.

Mix butter with peanut oil, cinnamon, and sugar. Brush pears with butter mixture.

Preheat stovetop grill. Cook pear quarters over medium-high heat for 1 minute on each side. Remove pear pieces, divide evenly, and place into 4 dessert dishes. Top with Coffee Liqueur Sauce. Pass extra sauce at table. Good served with coffee and small cookies.

Makes 4 servings

Chestnuts

**1 jar (8 oz) whole
  chestnuts, drained**
**4 8-inch bamboo
  skewers, soaked in
  water 10 minutes,
  drained**
**3 tablespoons butter or
  margarine, melted**
1 teaspoon orange zest

**2 cups heavy cream,
  whipped**
1 1/2 teaspoons vanilla
1/2 cup sugar

Thread chestnuts onto bamboo skewers. Mix melted butter with orange zest. Brush chestnuts with flavored butter. Set aside.

Spoon whipped cream into a bowl. Mix with vanilla and sugar. Divide cream into dessert dishes.

Preheat stovetop grill. Cook chestnuts over medium-high heat until warm, about 2 to 3 minutes. turning after each minute. Set each chestnut skewer over whipped cream.

Makes 4 servings

Honeydew Wedges with Berries

1 small ripe honeydew
3 tablespoons butter or
margarine, melted
2 tablespoons orange-
flavored liqueur
1 teaspoon orange zest

2 cups strawberries
Mint leaves, optional, for
garnish

Honeydew melons are incredibly sweet and juicy. The pale green color of the honeydew slices makes an elegant dessert when paired with the rich red of the strawberries.

Cut honeydew in half and discard seeds. Peel, using a paring knife. Cut melon into 3/4-inch wedges. Arrange melon on a plate.

Mix melted butter with liqueur and orange zest. Brush honeydew wedges with flavored butter.

Wash and hull strawberries. Pat dry with paper towels and slice. Refrigerate strawberries until ready to serve.

Preheat stovetop grill. Cook honeydew wedges over medium heat for 1 minute on each side. Remove to a serving dish. Scatter strawberries over warm melon wedges. Sprinkle with mint leaves, if desired. Serve immediately.

Makes 4 servings

Apple Rounds with
Cider Sabayon Sauce

■ Cider Sabayon Sauce

6 egg yolks
1/2 cup sugar
1/4 cup brandy
3/4 cup apple cider

4 ripe apples, such as
  Golden Delicious
2 tablespoons freshly
  squeezed lemon juice
1 cup sugar
1/2 teaspoon ground
  cinnamon
Melted butter or marga-
  rine, for brushing grill

This dessert is richer than most because of the sabayon sauce, which is traditionally a blend of egg yolks, wine, and sugar. In this recipe, however, I have used cider in place of wine.

To prepare sabayon sauce, bring water to a boil in bottom half of a double boiler over medium heat. Whisk together egg yolks, sugar, brandy, and cider in top half of double boiler. Reduce heat to simmer and set top half of boiler over the simmering water. Whisk sauce until it is foamy and has doubled in volume.

Peel and core apples and cut them into 1/2-inch rounds. Place apple slices in a bowl. Sprinkle with lemon juice. Mix sugar and cinnamon together and spread on a plate. Roll apple slices in sugar/cinnamon mixture.

Preheat stovetop grill. Brush grill surface with butter. Cook apple slices over medium heat for 1 minute on each side. Place apple slices on separate dessert dishes.

Spoon Cider Sabayon Sauce over apples. Serve immediately.

Makes 4 servings

INDEX